16

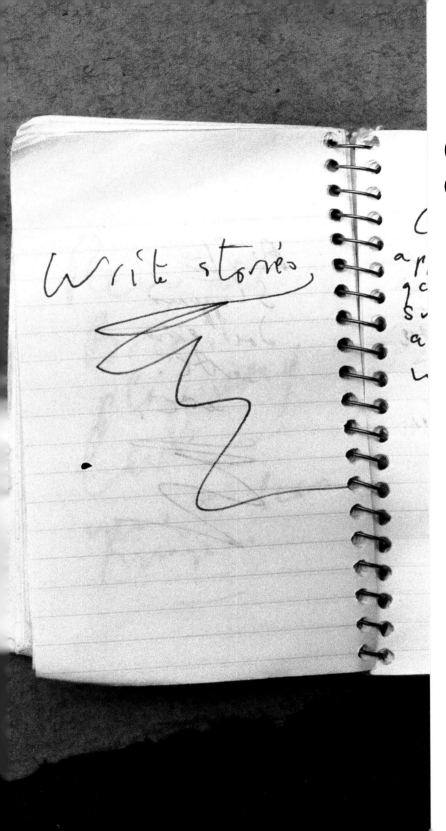

CARVER COUNTRY
The World of Raymond Carver

Texts by Raymond Carver

Photographs by Bob Adelman

Introduction by Ann Beattie

Afterword by Tess Gallagher

A Bob Adelman Book

The Quantuck Lane Press
New York

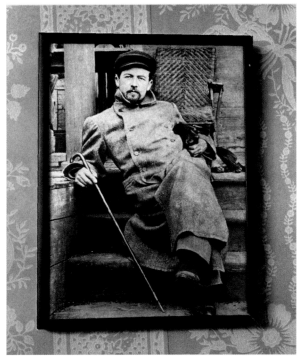

Preceding pages: Raymond Carver's desk in Syracuse, New York. (1984)
Above: Photograph of Anton Chekhov, on the wall in Carver's study in Syracuse, New York. (1984)
Opposite: Carver's study in the house in Syracuse, New York. (1984)

Text by Tess Gallagher Copyright © 2013.
Photographs by Bob Adelman Copyright © 2013.
Introduction by Ann Beattie Copyright © 2013
Carver chronology and bibliography by William L. Stull and Maureen P. Carroll Copyright © 2013.

Library of Congress Cataloging-in-Publication Data
Carver, Raymond, 1938-1988.
 Carver Country : the World of Raymond Carver / texts by Raymond Carver ; photographs by Bob Adelman ; introduction by Ann Beattie ; afterword by Tess Gallagher.
     pages cm
 "A Bob Adelman Book."
 Includes bibliographical references.
 ISBN 978-1-59372-053-7
1. Carver, Raymond, 1938-1988—Correspondence. 2. Carver, Raymond, 1938-1988—Homes and haunts—Pictorial works. 3. Authors, American—20th century—Correspondence. 4. United States—Intellectual life—20th century. I. Adelman, Bob, photographer. II. Title.
PS3553.A7894Z48 2013
813'.54--dc23
 [B]
                    2012040776
Manufacturing by C&C Offset Printing Co.

Printed in China

Originally published as A Robert Stewart Book by Charles Scribner's Sons.

1 2 3 4 5 6 7 8 9 0

Design by Rick DeMonico
Editing by Mary A. Dempsey
Digital Scans by Christopher Cataldo and Stephen Watt

"Cathedral", "Where I'm Calling From", "Vitamins", "Chef's House", "Feathers" from *Cathedral* by Raymond Carver, copyright © 1981, 1982, 1983 by Raymond Carver. Used by permission of Alfred A. Knopf, a division of Random House, Inc. "Gazebo" from *What We Talk About When We Talk About Love* by Raymond Carver, copyright © 1974, 1976, 1978, 1980, 1981 by Raymond Carver. Used by permission of Alfred A. Knopf, a division of Random House, Inc. "The Car", "The Phone Booth", from *Ultramarine* by Raymond Carver, copyright © 1986 by Raymond Carver. Used by permission of Random House, Inc. "My Boat", "Where Water Comes Together with Other Water", "Elk Camp", "To My Daughter", "For Tess", "In a Marine Light near Sequim, Washington", from *Where Water Comes Together With Other Water* by Raymond Carver. Used by permission of Random House, Inc. Any third party use of this material, outside of this publication, is prohibited. Interested parties must apply directly to Random House, Inc. for permission. "Miracle," "The Kitchen," "Hummingbird," "Gravy," "After-glow," "Late Fragment" from *A New Path to the Waterfall*, copyright © 1989 by the Estate of Raymond Carver. Used by permission of Grove/Atlantic, Inc. Excerpts from "Boxes" and "Menudo" from *Where I'm Calling From*, copyright © 1988 by Raymond Carver. Used by permission of Grove/Atlantic, Inc. Any third party use of this material, outside of this publication, is prohibited.

The Quantuck Lane Press, New York
www.quantucklanepress.com

Distributed by W. W. Norton & Company,
500 Fifth Avenue, New York, NY 10110
www.wwnorton.com

W. W. Norton & Company Ltd.
Castle House, 75/76 Wells Street, London, WIT 3QT

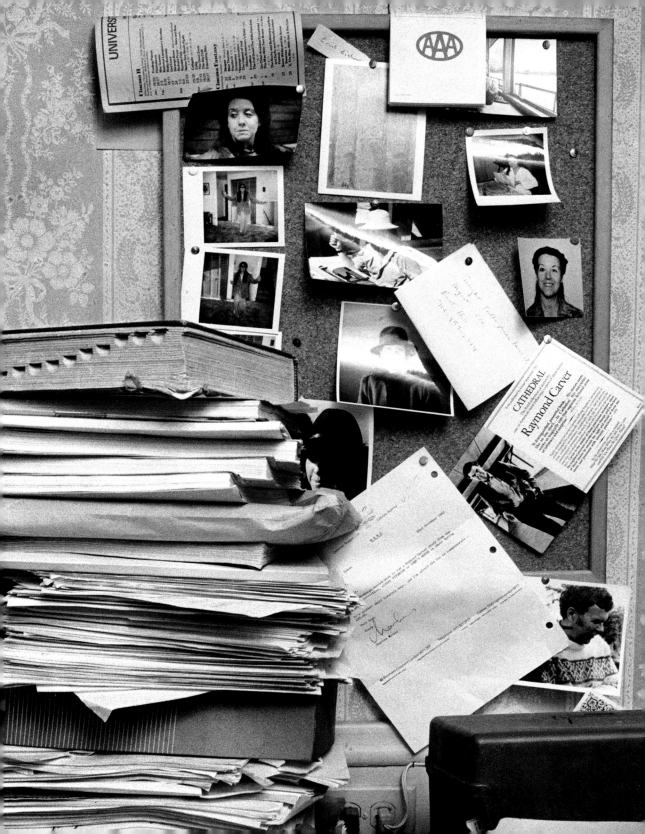

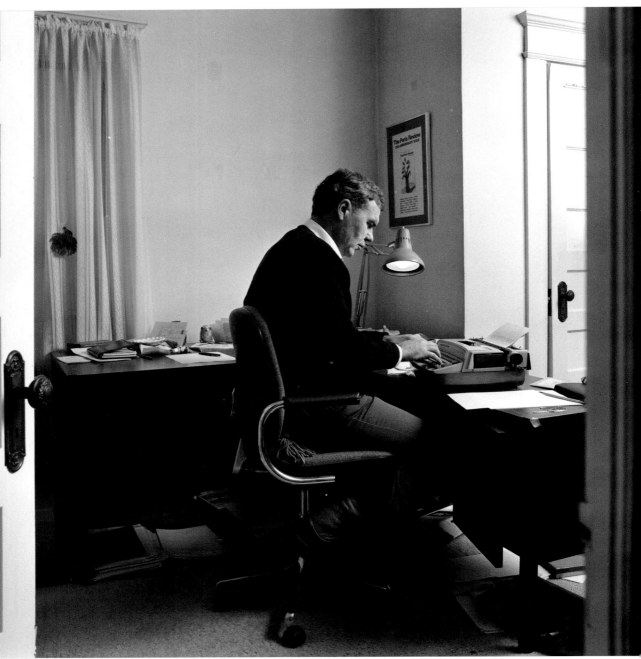

Carver at work, Syracuse, New York. (1984)

Contents

Introduction
by
Ann Beattie

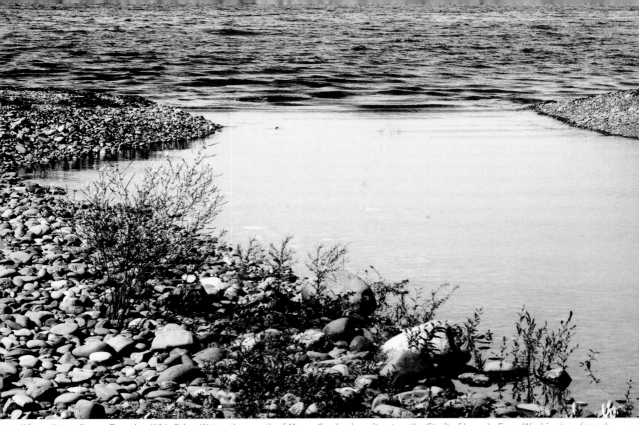

Where Water Comes Together With Other Water, the mouth of Morse Creek where it enters the Strait of Juan de Fuca, Washington. (2007)

Raymond Carver, so often willingly or unwillingly the center of so many interpersonal dramas, was also a modest man who had a great talent. We have his essays that attest to the difficulty of supporting a family and also finding time to write; we have the evidence — so well-known, I don't need to re-state it — about his alcoholism, his quitting drinking, and his eventually becoming one of the acknowledged masters of the short story. At least at the time, it seemed he was the anointed Great Story Writer. If he had detractors, they weren't his fellow writers. He was appreciated, admired, in many cases loved. I can't believe Tess Gallagher would have held any different opinion, even if they'd never married. He had a reputation for excellence among writers long before the New Yorker published him, or the New York Times Book Review gave him such a big thumbs-up that anyone reading the praise might have looked upward to see if you-know-who was beaming down agreement. All enthusiasm deserved, his mixture of talent and magic still not taken for granted in even the most perceptive and appreciative reader's minds. He beat the odds; he beat the system (he never wrote a novel; he was a poet and short story writer who was most praised for his stories); he didn't beat death, but his poems suggest that he didn't expect to, either. Also, that he hugely valued what he'd had. On the personal level, it had come at quite a price. On the professional, his talent had come to astonish almost anyone who came in contact with him, including editors and publishers.

Mark Doty, writing about Elizabeth Bishop's brilliant poem, "The Fish," says, "When our imagination meets a mind [the fish's mind] decidedly not like ours, our own nature is suddenly called into question." Of course this can be disconcerting. Even embarrassing. But if we've taken the plunge, why not get from the experience what we can? After all, we wear costumes on Halloween, or dress up for parties, or even just to impress. Carver's characters, however, were fish. They were what they obviously were: waitresses, or enigmatic fat men ordering way too much food from those waitresses, or people about to declare bankruptcy the next day. Still, in the ordinary resided convoluted insights and truths, though we had to get down there, get to the level of the fish, who were only inhabiting their natural world, to see something from their perspective. That's what short stories do. They don't attempt to convince you that a character is right or wrong, most of the time (though of course they allow those of us so inclined to rush to judgment); instead, they ask readers to inhabit the minds and bodies of some pretty unlikely characters, who are nevertheless recognizable enough that they might act as temporary guides to something that shimmers right in front of us that we don't know, or have neglected to acknowledge. In this finality of awareness, poems seem more related to stories than to novels — so it's interesting that Carver wrote in both genres. The novel has no less lofty intentions, but chronological time can allow us to let ourselves off the hook: sure, something that is gradually revealed can still have an enormous impact, but if it devolved over time, time alone can soothe the realization. It's the compactness of a story that asks for so much from the reader, so quickly. The reader will only have a brief amount of time to spend in a character's company, and even if the story can be re-read, all attention must be given from the first to the reality or lack of reality of the situation. The implicit question is: where do you, the reader, stand in relationship to this? Because as Flannery O'Connor trenchantly observed, "The average reader is pleased to observe anybody's wooden leg being stolen." We're not reading for edification, or to figure out how to live our lives. We're reading to see where we stand vis a vis the characters, whether if we had a wooden leg, we'd behave like O'Connor's character; whether if we were declaring bankruptcy, we'd have made the frightening unspoken pact Carver's Toni and Leo have in "Are These Actual Miles?" So many short stories contain a world of worries and pain. Sometimes, even worlds of high hilarity and bravado. But Carver positions himself elsewhere. His fascination is with the real and the probable (even if we only recognize that in retrospect); his devices are many, including humor, matter-of-factness (ask any good comedian how important this is), brevity to the point of suggesting to the reader a panicked descent into projected, imagined depths (as did Beckett).

If you are familiar with his work, you will already know this, and much more. You will not have heard his exact tone before, and we haven't heard it again. There has been ample time for imitation or for continuing on a path he cleared. That has happened, sometimes wonderfully well, even advantageously. But he was the first one out there with a particular vision, not only of his characters, but with the implication — the faith — that the reader could be guided toward figuring out what shivered and shuddered below the surface, when reading individual stories. Because they wouldn't exist if you didn't.

How risky. But it worked.

When you look at Bob Adelman's photographs — sometimes of the writer himself, other times of the glaringly inauspicious (I know it's a paradox) settings where he based his stories, or from which he derived his inspiration — you'll see a rather anonymous world that has been made so particular by Carver's visitation, we can no longer just turn away from its bleak, formulaic postcard façade. Bob and Ray certainly shared an odd sense of humor, though neither makes easy jokes at the perceiver's expense. f these people and places don't exactly announce themselves, remember that Carver himself warmed to them as subject matter slowly, often conflicted about approach or avoidance, which he incorporated, ultimately, into his stories.

To recognize the extraordinary in the ordinary is a much-commended pursuit. To make something ordinary yours, even after it really has been yours, much less typical, simply because it's so difficult to separate yourself from it. My reading of Carver's stories makes me yearn not so much for a de-coding of the actual versus the possible or the imaginary; instead, I want to think I've sunk to the bottom (or close to it, oftentimes) with Carver, who gives me clues, but who shows me around a little, then soon absents himself. Which leaves me with the story. And with myself. These photographs are a good point of departure, too, a reference, an unlikely stage set for a performance. Notice the respect with which author and photographer move. I see where I am, but where are each of them in the picture? (They can be found.)

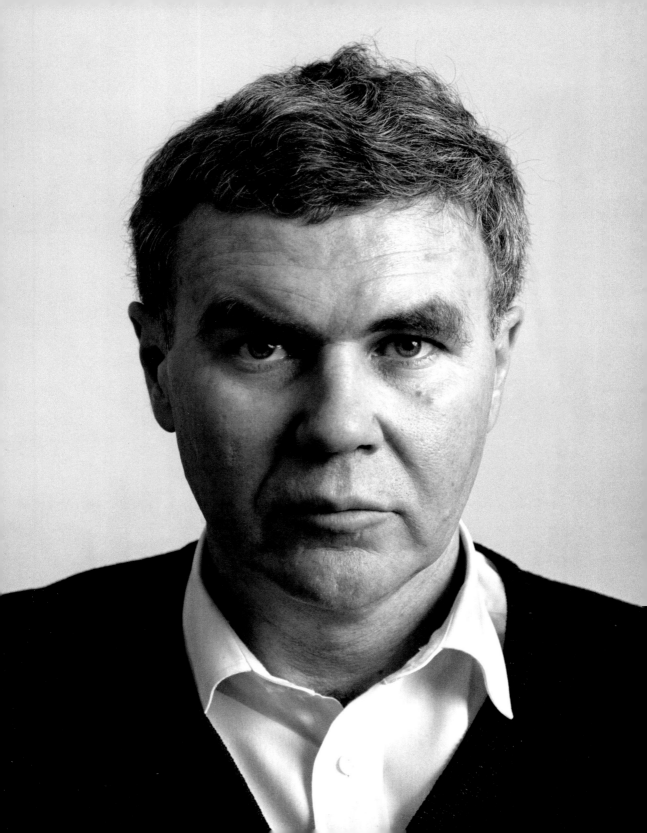

Dear Bob,

Well, I'll be glad to see your smiling face out in Port Angeles. And it won't be long now. I talked to Ford last night, who is back in Missoula, and he said you were coming to visit him Dec. 21st—at least I think I recall that as the date. I'll be glad to be able to see him and talk to him about his week long stay in Hollywood; I think he has a few adventure stories to tell. . . .

I'm going to try and run through some places and towns and people, and this will be in no particular order or grouping, and it will be the more difficult since I don't have a map even of the state of Washington or Oregon. So I will just start off with, say, Yakima, and move around there and its environs, and then move on to another location, but may come back to Yakima if I can recall something else along the way. . . . Not a very specific way to work, I know, but we're not scientists, and what the hell.

First address I clearly remember in Yakima is down by the fairgrounds, and is now a slum area; and the actual house I lived in has burned down—or at least there was nothing left but an old shell of a house a couple of years ago. The address is 1515 So. 15th St. As I recall, the road in front of the house that leads to the "main" road is not even paved; the people who live there in the neighborhood now look like people out of the Virginia backwoods. They'll look at you very strangely, esp. if you're driving a nice car and carrying an expensive camera!

The fairgrounds itself is worth seeing. It's been modernized a lot now, since those olden days, but I used to spend a lot of time over there hanging out around the deserted barns and such.

Raymond Carver, Syracuse, New York. (1984)

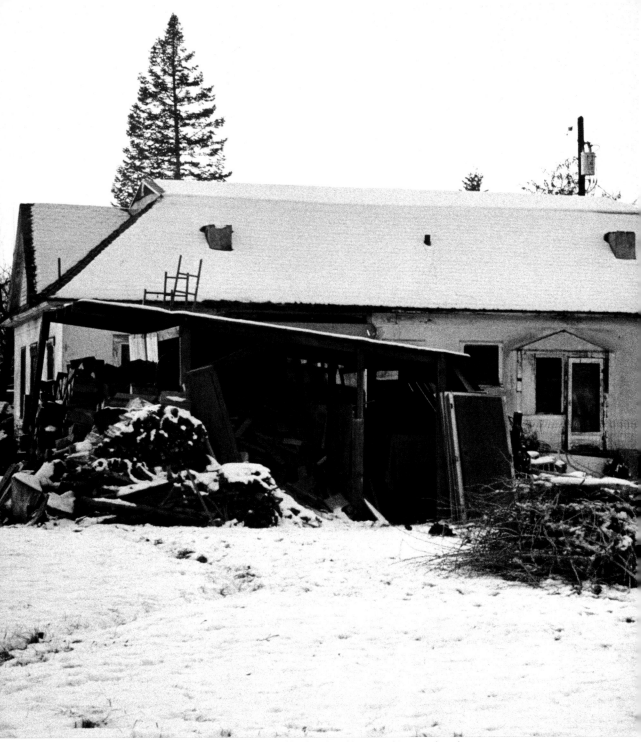

Naches Avenue neighborhood, Yakima, Washington. (1987)

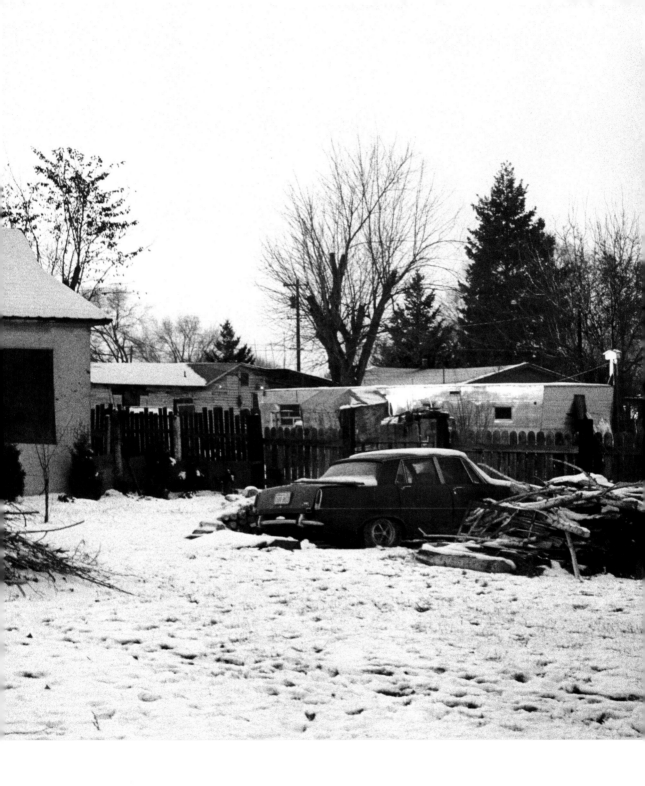

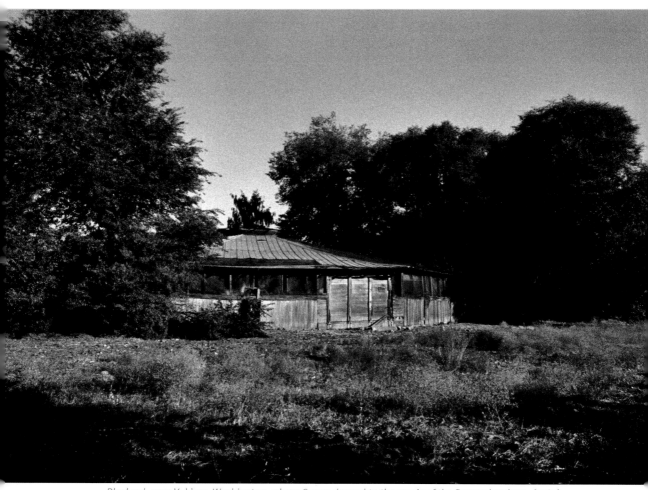

Playland, near Yakima, Washington, where Carver danced to the music of the Dorsey brothers. (1989)

Then there is a bridge across the Yakima River, not too far from the 1515 So. 15th St. address. My dad and I used to walk from our house to the river to fish, and sometimes we would walk all the way to what is called Sportsmen's Park. (It was called Sportsmen's Park in those days, too, it was just wilder then—not so developed.) But I have set a recent unpublished poem there; and then I cut back to the So. 15th St. house. I also fell off a raft there when I was a kid, and cut my leg so badly I had to be taken to a hospital. (40 stitches it was right down to the tendons.) We had no car, my dad and I, so we had to flag down a ride. There is also a town about 8 or 10 miles away called Moxee. I had a girlfriend from there once upon a time. Then, on a New Year's eve, I took her on a date, a dance at a place called Playland, out toward Selah, Wash. (on the other side of Yakima, and some remnants of Playland are still there), and I got horribly drunk, really drunk, for the first time, and I passed out cold, and people thought I had died. She called me up the next day and said it was over between us! (I can't imagine why she would want to adopt this drastic attitude!) There are also some extraordinarily beautiful, I think, hop fields across the river, heading toward Moxee. Hops don't grow, for some reason, in very many places, but the Yakima Valley is one of those places. I picked hops for a while, one summer. Unimaginably hard work.

Another important address there is on 11th Avenue... I can't give you the exact address, but it is five houses down from a street called Mead Avenue (on righthand side of street)... directly behind the house is a Pentecostal church of some sort... All these little houses look and are alike, all the houses on this part of 11th Avenue. But it is this house where I spent much of my growing years and used to walk to the fishing holes at Bachelor Creek, right near the airport in Yakima. (The story "Nobody Said Anything" is set right here, in this house, and I actually give pretty good directions from walking to Bachelor Creek from that house on 11th Avenue.) I also fished a creek near the airport called Athanum Creek, and another little creek in there whose name I forget right now. Athanum Creek goes way up into the valley, toward Indian

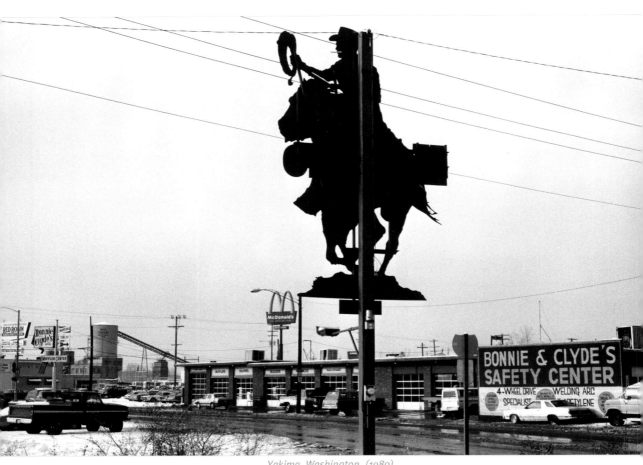

Yakima, Washington. (1989)

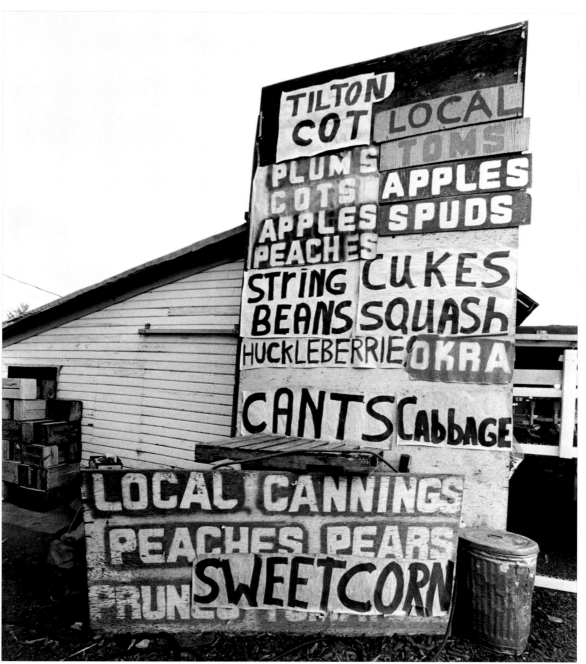

Yakima, Washington. (1989)

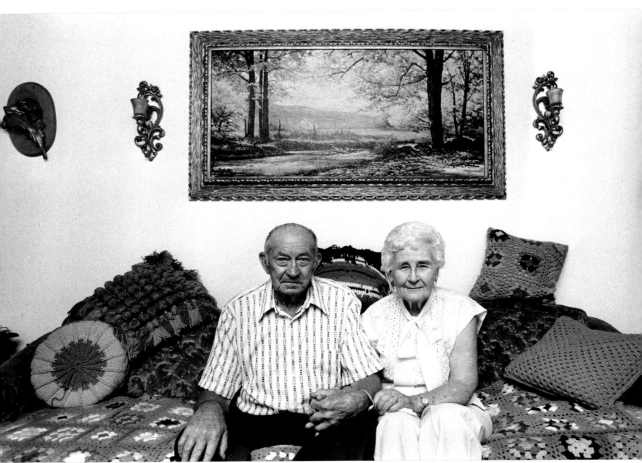

Bill and Vonda Archer, Carver's aunt and uncle, with whom he often stayed with as a boy. (1989)

reservation country, and beautiful farm land, running alongside the hills, and it is very beautiful. I fished near the fish hatchery at Bachelor Creek—the road crosses the creek there, near the hatchery, and you can park and fish—or photograph!

Another place is Wenas Lake, Wenas Creek, up in the valley beyond Selah, ten or 15 miles. I don't have any idea what it's like up there now, but we hunted and fished there.

People in Yakima: my dear old aunt and uncle, Bill and Vonda Archer. My ex-sister-in-law, Jerry Davis, Maryann's older sister, who I am still in touch with and who is like an older sister to me. She knows a lot about my early life and is a good woman and would be happy to be photographed or talked to or whatever. (She also figures in a story or two of mine.) Another man who figures in a story and a poem, but I don't even know if he is still alive, though he is a tough old geezer, and probably is. His name is Frank Sandmeyer and he lives on Queen Street, or Queen Avenue, over near the 11th Avenue place. I used to fish and hunt with him and looked up to him as an expert in those matters. Don't take "No" for an answer from him—if you should contact him and he should say no.

The last place I lived in with my parents in Yakima, and this was just before I graduated and just before my dad moved to California to take another job, got sick, and their lives blew apart: this was 1501 Summitview, and it was the best house they had ever lived in and ever were to live in. It was downhill all the way after that; trailers, apts., shacks, cabins, and with other people.

There is a tiny Episcopal church on Yakima Avenue and Naches Avenue in downtown Yakima. I went to funeral services for a high school friend killed in a car wreck there one day, and the next day Maryann and I were married in this same church. St. James or St. Michael's church…

Places away from Yakima: some of the most beautiful country in the world, to my way of thinking, is what people called the "Horse Heaven" country, up over the hills from, say, Prosser, Washington.

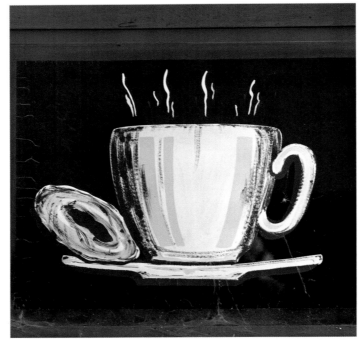

Ye Olde Donut Shoppe, a Carver hangout in Yakima, Washington. (1989)

The Sports Center, downtown Yakima, Washington. (1989)

10

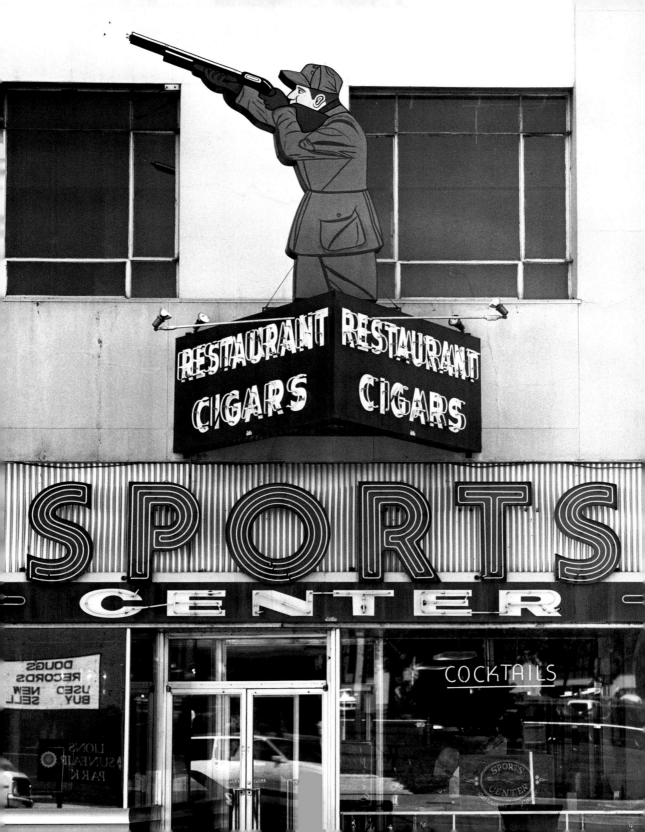

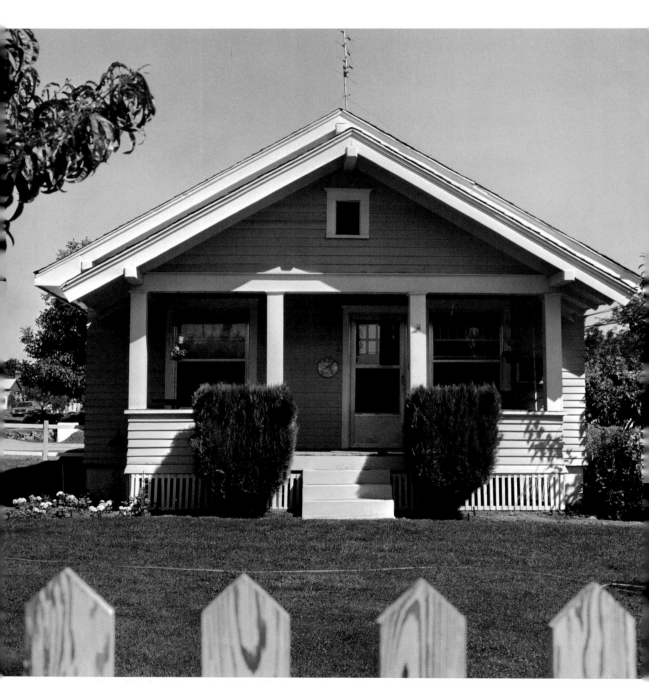

One of the family houses in Yakima, Washington; Carver remembered it his best boyhood home. (1989)

(I have a poem called "Prosser," as you know, in FIRES.) Anyway, it is wheat country, or at least it was then, running all the way to the Columbia River, near the McNary Dam. But the highway out of Prosser will take you up into the wheat country and all the way to the river. There used to be bluffs along the river—there is a creek I'm thinking of called Alder Creek, and the Alder Creek canyon—and we would hide in blinds up on those bluffs and shoot geese when they passed over us. Beautiful country, and it was very wild in those days. Lots of deer and bobcats, partridge, even cougar... I wrote a poem about seeing a cougar called "The Cougar"—I think it too is in FIRES. Anyway, sometimes we would go to Mabton, Washington, and turn there and head for the Columbia River that way. Goldendale was a town, is a town, that time forgot. It sits in the wheat country way up over the Columbia River—you can see far over into the mts. of Oregon—and then down below Goldendale, on the Columbia River, on a hill overlooking the river, is the strangest museum in the world, called the Mayhill Museum. You must see this if you get down there in that part of the country. The Queen of Rumania or some such dignitary visited there, maybe dedicated the place, back in the 1920s. And there is a sign next to the museum, planted right in the middle of the green grass, that says, Caution—Don't walk on grass as there are rattlesnakes here—or something, some warning like that. It's quite a place. And the town and river of Klickitat.

If you are driving from Missoula, you will have to cross the Columbia River at Vantage, Washington. My parents and I used to go there to fish for whitefish, and sometimes we stayed overnight in a little cabin there, a tourist court cabin... I have a poem abt. this place, Vantage, Wash., and am presently using it as a setting for a story I'm messing around with. Ellensburg is midway between Vantage and Yakima, but Ellensburg never figured much in my life. But take the highway that parallels the Yakima River into Yakima, not the new superhighway that goes over the hills, and nothing to see there but ugly terrain. But take the old old highway that runs along-side the river, for the most part. I fished and hunted up and

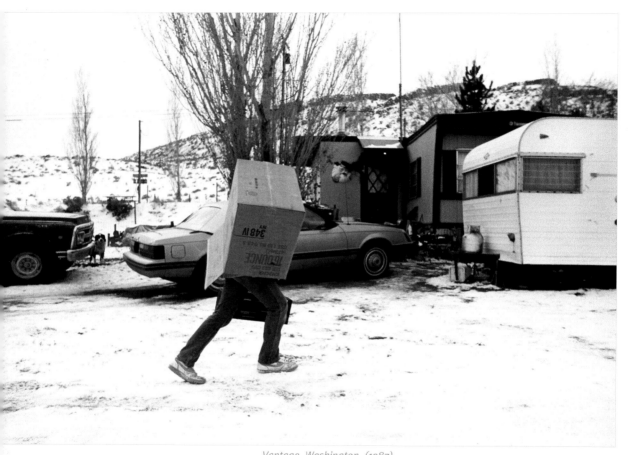

Vantage, Washington. (1987)

On the way to Wenas Ridge, Washington. (1987)

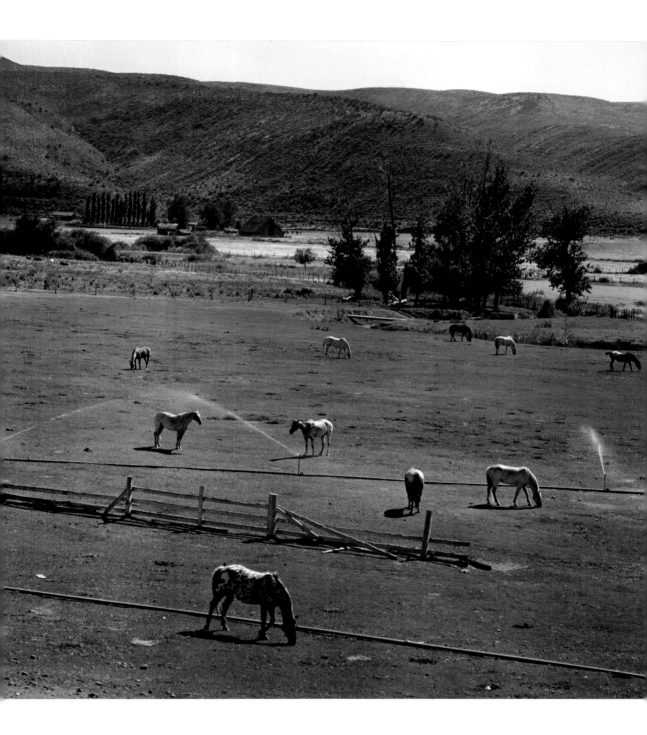

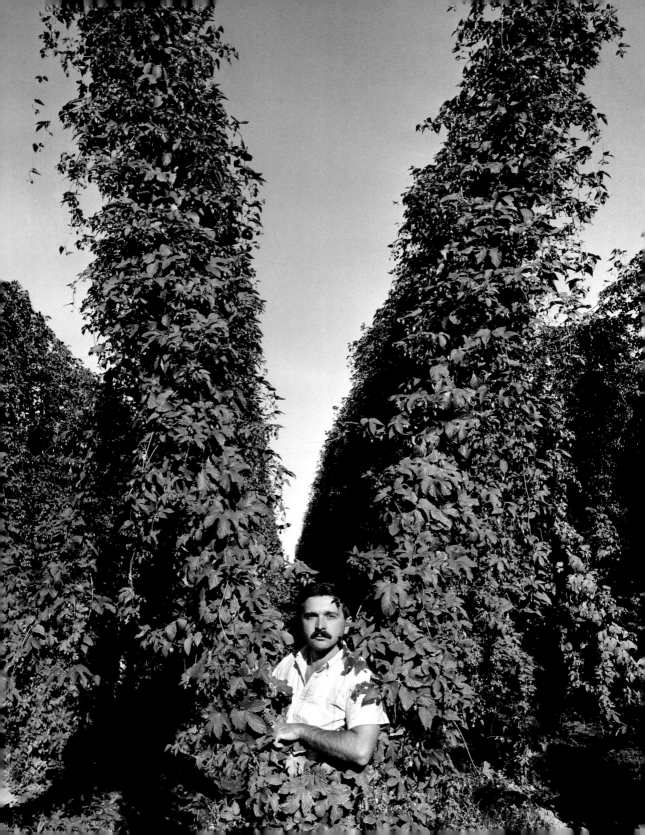

down that river a hundred times I could put a caption, or write a few lines about any spot on that river that you might want to photograph... You would probably have to go into downtown Ellensburg to pick up the old highway; don't follow the interstate highway signs to Yakima... Go into Ellensburg and take the old highway to Yakima—about 30 minutes longer, that's all, I think.

The Bonneville Dam on the Columbia River is an important place to me. I've stopped there every time I've passed for the past 30 years. It's an extraordinary place now, with fish ladders, underground and underwater viewing rooms; the dam and locks themselves, the sturgeon pond and trout ponds in the parklike area before you get to the locks and ladders... Biggs Junction is a town, in Oregon, where people used to have to cross the river by ferry, I'm not kidding. When Maryann and I first went to California, back in 1957, we crossed the river in our car by ferry. But mainly my part of the river, where I hunted, was from Roosevelt or Arlington, Washington (one of those towns is, I believe, across the river in Oregon, the other is in Washington), up the river past Alder Creek, several miles on up the river to where the highway branches off and goes off toward Prosser. And all that gorgeous wheat country in beyond there, back of those bluffs. There are probably lots of roads in and out of there now, but there weren't in those days.

Back to the Yakima area. There is something called Esbach Park (sp.?) on the Naches River where I used to spend time. And not far from there, on the highway out of Yakima going toward Mt. Rainier, Chinook Pass and White Pass, the highway crosses over the Naches River. Right there, up on your left (I think the whole area is marked now by signs), is something called Painted Rocks—it's where I set my story "Tell the Women We're Going." And there is the little town of Gleed, and Naches itself, and the Tieton River where I used to fish, and hunt for grouse, and the place I had in mind for my poem "Wenas Ridge," though the events that happened in that poem happened in a little canyon up off the Tieton River and not in the Wenas Lake, or Creek, area.

Thomas Suave, a hop farmer, near Yakima, Washington. (1989)

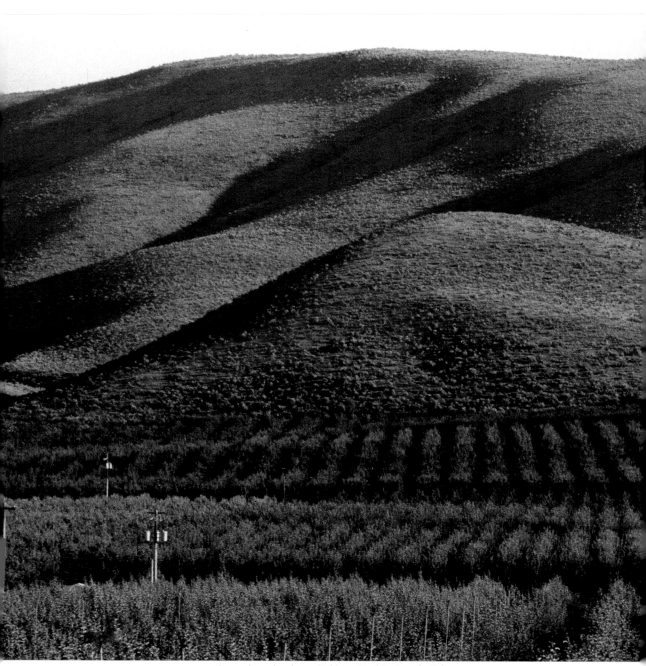

An apple orchard near Yakima, Washington. (1989)

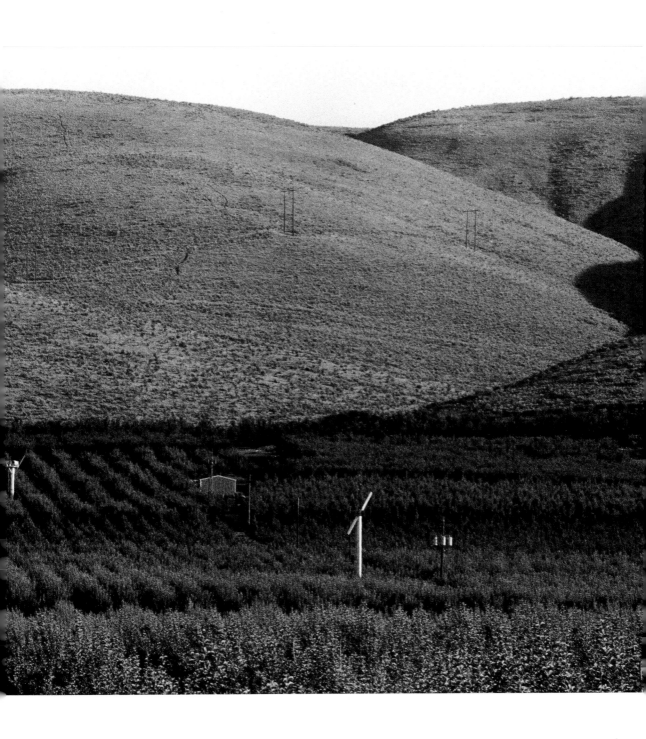

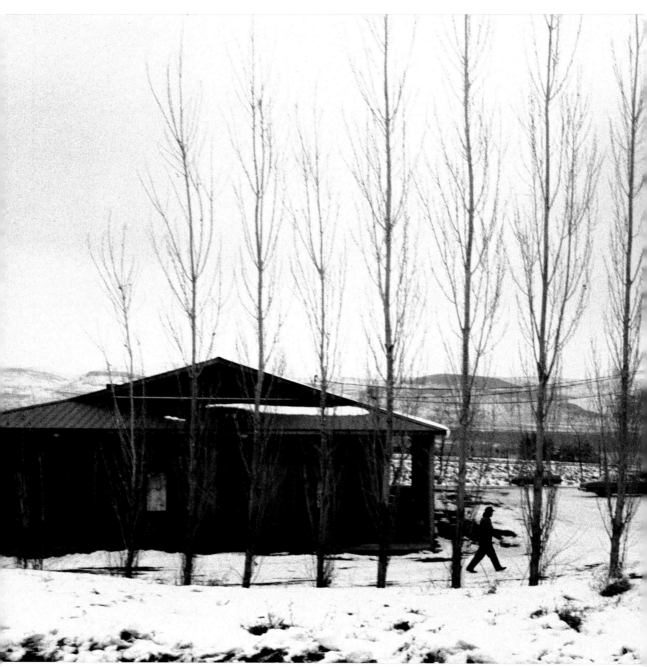

Vantage, Washington. (1987)

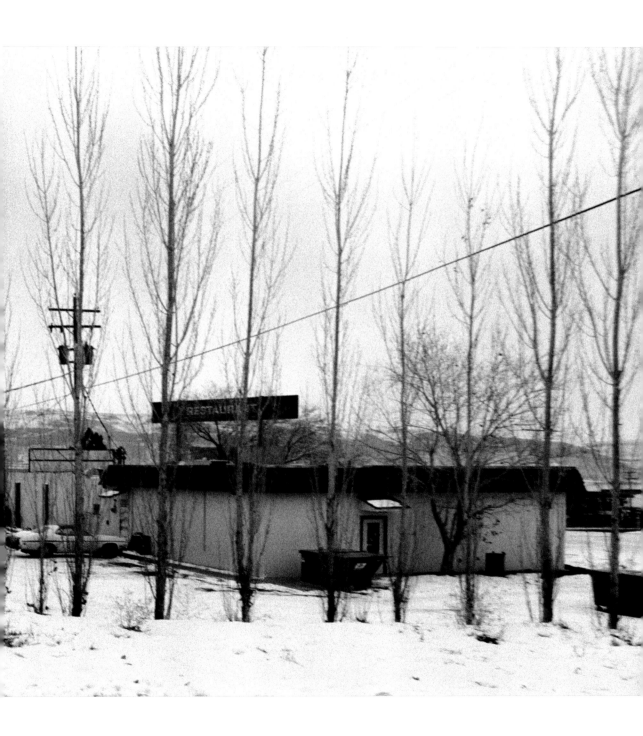

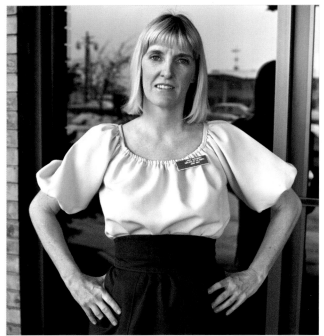

Employee of the Month at the Red Lion Inn, Yakima, Washington. (1989)

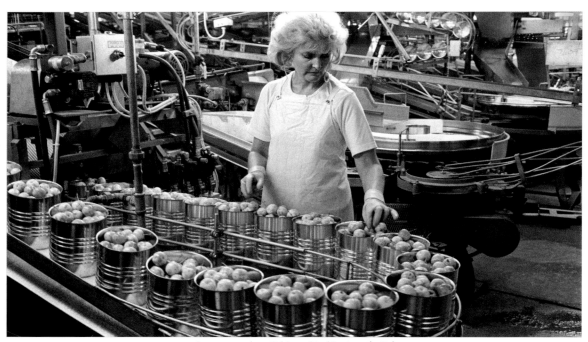

Cannery worker, Yakima, Washington. (1989)

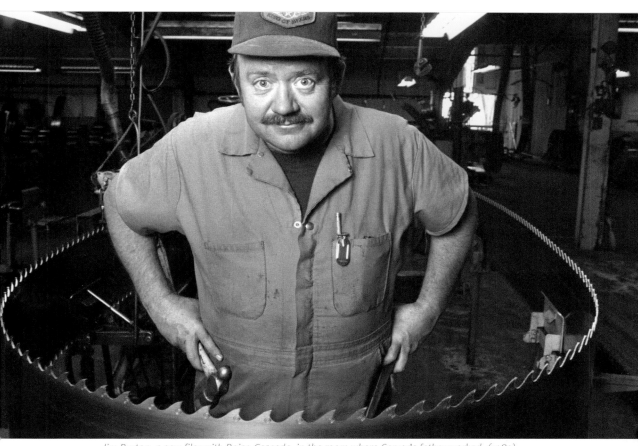

Jim Burton, a saw filer with Boise-Cascade, in the room where Carver's father worked. (1989)

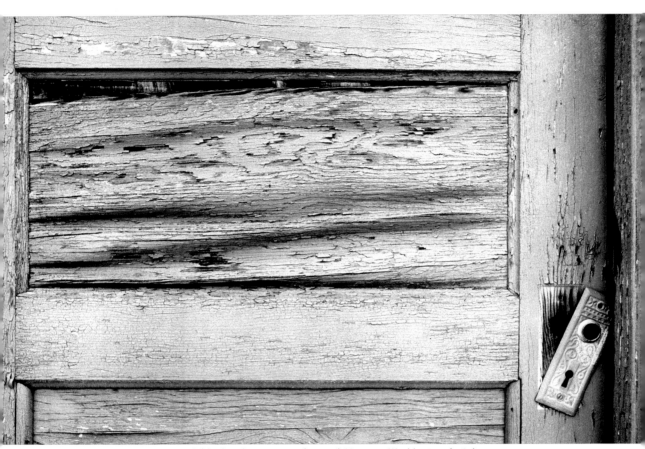

Cabin door in a 1950s-style motel, Vantage, Washington. (1987)

You'll see, when you see Yakima, if you drive around at all, in the Naches Avenue area, or just about anywhere, in the North 3rd and Fourth Street areas, that in many ways it's as if time stood still, or stopped, back in the 1950s. And, you must take a look at the Boise-Cascade Lumber company—if it's still called that; in those days it was just the Cascade Lumber Co., and all of my father's male family members worked there, and their friends and that was my entire frame of reference when I was a kid… My God, if the mill is still there, please take a picture or two of it. And Sportsmen's Park, for sure.

You might see a hundred other things you want to photograph, and that's fine, I'll probably recognize them when I see them.

I'll close this off for now. If and when you want to ever do the Arcata-Eureka part of things, tell me. But for sheer pictorial interest, and so on, the pictures and text of the early days in the Yakima Valley area, and the poems and stories that fit in there, that seems of more interest, finally. What do you think?

I mean, as you know, I lived in Chico, Sacramento, San Francisco, San Jose, Palo Alto, Cupertino, Sunnyvale, etc., etc. But those times were different, very different, from those earlier, more "innocent" days. Anyway, we can talk further about this later.

Give a call if needs be, or if anything here is unclear. Otherwise, we look forward to seeing you on the morning of the 26th in Port Angeles. Call B. St. house first, which is probably where we'll be staying, or else Tess's house. We can plan to start work early that Saturday morning; as Tess probably told you, we have to go to Seattle late in the afternoon… Write or phone, or let Richard know where you will be staying in Pt. Angeles—the Red Lion Inn is a good convenient location; I think you stayed there before—we'll check in with each other the night of Dec. 25th.

In haste, but with love,

Ray

Ruined saw blades on the wall in the saw filer room at Boise-Cascade. (1989)

From "My Father's Life"

In Omak, Washington, my dad and mother lived in a little place not much bigger than a cabin. My grandparents lived next door. My dad was still working on the dam, and later, with the huge turbines producing electricity and the water backed up for a hundred miles into Canada, he stood in the crowd and heard Franklin D. Roosevelt when he spoke at the construction site. "He never mentioned those guys who died building that dam," my dad said. Some of his friends had died there, men from Arkansas, Oklahoma, and Missouri.

He then took a job in a sawmill in Clatskanie, Oregon, a little town alongside the Columbia River. I was born there, and my mother has a picture of my dad standing in front of the gate to the mill proudly holding me up to face the camera. My bonnet is on crooked and about to come untied. His hat is pushed back on his forehead, and he's wearing a big grin. Was he going in to work or just finishing his shift? It doesn't matter. In either case, he had a job and a family. These were his salad days.

In 1941 we moved to Yakima, Washington, where my dad went to work as a saw filer, a skilled trade he'd learned in Clatskanie. When war broke out, he was given a deferment because his work was considered necessary to the war effort. Finished lumber was in demand by the armed services, and he kept his saws so sharp they could shave the hair off your arm.

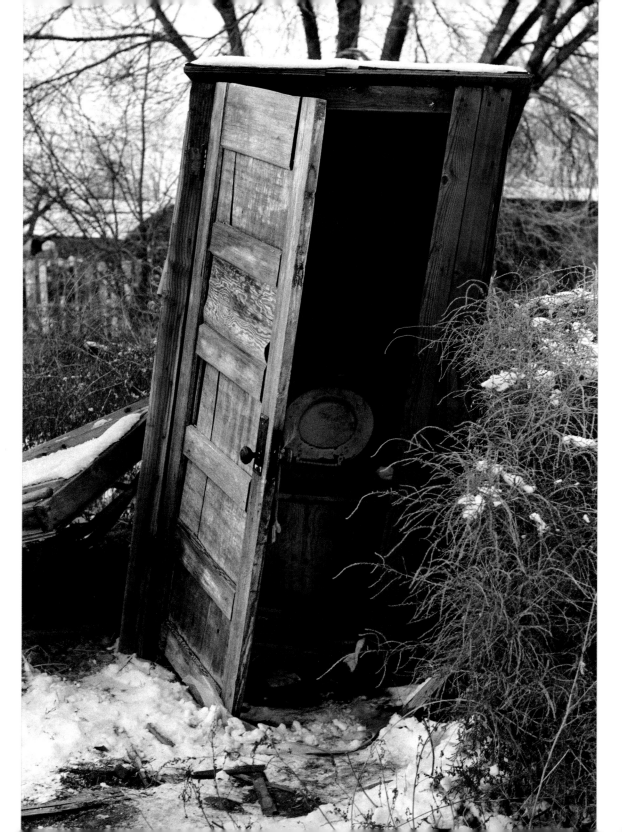

From "My Father's Life"

The first house I clearly remember living in, at 1515 South Fifteenth Street, in Yakima, had an outdoor toilet. On Halloween night, or just any night, for the hell of it, neighbor kids, kids in their early teens, would carry our toilet away and leave it next to the road. My dad would have to get somebody to help him bring it home. Or these kids would take the toilet and stand it in somebody else's backyard. Once they actually set it on fire. But ours wasn't the only house that had an outdoor toilet. When I was old enough to know what I was doing, I threw rocks at the other toilets when I'd see someone go inside. This was called bombing the toilets. After a while, though, everyone went to indoor plumbing until, suddenly, our toilet was the last outdoor one in the neighborhood. I remember the shame I felt when my third-grade teacher, Mr. Wise, drove me home from school one day. I asked him to stop at the house just before ours, claiming I lived there.

The outhouse at 1515 South 15th Street, Yakima, Washington. (1989)

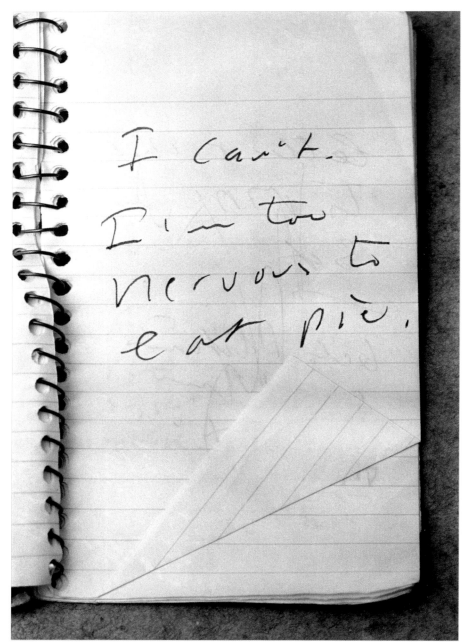

Carver's notebook. (1989)

Lines Of Reference

From a 1983 interview for *The Paris Review*

The fiction I'm most interested in has lines of reference to the real world. None of my stories really happened, of course. But there's always something, some element, something said to me or that I witnessed, that may be the starting place. Here's an example: "That's the last Christmas you'll ever ruin for us!" I was drunk when I heard that, but I remembered it. And later, much later, when I was sober, using only that one line and other things I imagined, imagined so accurately that they could have happened, I made a story—"A Serious Talk." But the fiction I'm most interested in, whether it's Tolstoy's fiction, Chekhov, Barry Hannah, Richard Ford, Hemingway, Isaac Babel, Ann Beattie, or Anne Tyler, strikes me as autobiographical to some extent. At the very least it's referential. Stories long or short don't just come out of thin air. I'm reminded of a conversation involving John Cheever. We were sitting around a table in Iowa City with some people and he happened to remark that after a family fracas at his home one night, he got up the next morning and went into the bathroom to find something his daughter had written in lipstick on the bathroom mirror: "D-e-r-e- daddy, don't leave us." Someone at the table spoke up and said, "I recognize that from one of your stories." Cheever said, "Probably so. Everything I write is autobiographical." Now of course that's not literally true. But everything we write is, in some way, autobiographical. I'm not in the least bothered by "autobiographical" fiction. To the contrary. *On the Road.* Celine. Roth. Lawrence Durrell in *The Alexandria Quartet.* So much of Hemingway in the Nick Adams stories. Updike, too, you bet. Jim McConkey. Clark Blaise is a contemporary writer whose fiction is out-and-out autobiography. Of course, you have to know what you're doing when you turn your life's stories into fiction. You have to be immensely daring, very skilled and imaginative and willing to tell everything on yourself. You're told time and again when you're young to write about what you know, and what do you know better than your own secrets? But, unless you're a special kind of writer, and a very talented one, it's dangerous to try and write volume after volume on The Story of My Life. A great danger, or at least a great temptation, for many writers is to become too autobiographical in their approach to their fiction. A little autobiography and a lot of imagination are best.

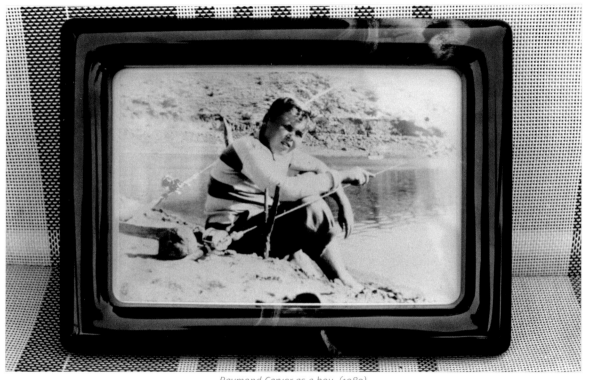

Raymond Carver as a boy. (1989)

Bobber

On the Columbia River near Vantage,
Washington, we fished for whitefish
in the winter months; my dad, Swede—
Mr. Lindgren—and me. They used belly-reels,
pencil-length sinkers, red, yellow, or brown
flies baited with maggots.
They wanted distance and went clear out there
to the edge of the riffle.
I fished near shore with a quill bobber and a cane pole.

My dad kept his maggots alive and warm
under his lower lip. Mr. Lindgren didn't drink.
I liked him better than my dad for a time.
He let me steer his car, teased me
about my name "Junior," and said
one day I'd grow into a fine man, remember
all this, and fish with my own son.
But my dad was right. I mean
he kept silent and looked into the river,
worked his tongue, like a thought, behind the bait.

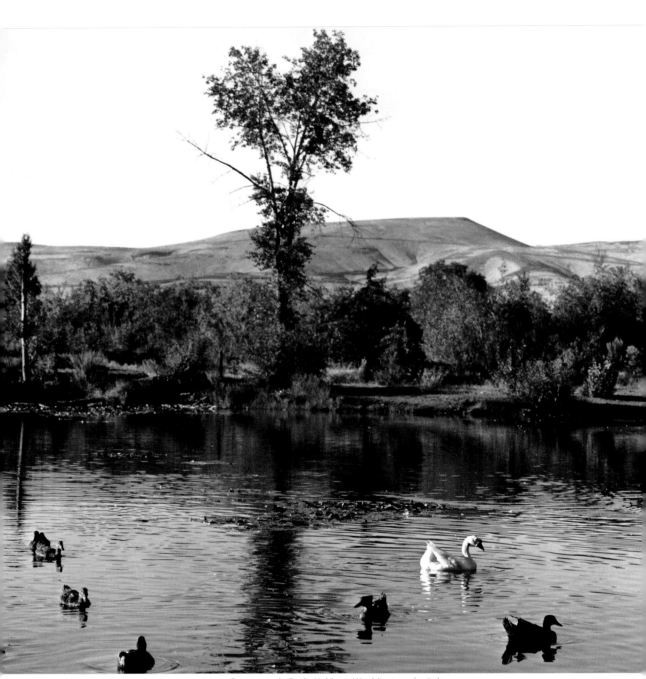

Sportsmen's Park, Yakima, Washington. (1989)

The Kitchen

At Sportsmen's Park, near Yakima, I crammed a hook
with worms, then cast it toward the middle
of the pond, hoping for bass. Bullfrogs scraped the air
invisibly. A turtle, flapjack-sized, slid
from a lily pad while another pulled itself onto
the same pad, a little staging area. Blue sky, warm
afternoon. I pushed a forked branch
into the sandy bank, rested the pole in the fork,
watched the bobber for a while, then beat off.
Grew sleepy then and let my eyes close.
Maybe I dreamed. I did that back then. When
suddenly, in my sleep, I heard a plop, and my eyes
flew open. My pole was gone!
I saw it tearing a furrow through
the scummy water. The bobber appeared, then
disappeared, then showed itself once more
skimming the surface, then gone under again.
What could I do? I bellowed, and bellowed some more.
Began to run along the bank, swearing to God
I would not touch myself again if He'd let me
retrieve that pole, that fish. Of course
there was no answer, not a sign.
I hung around the pond a long time
(the same pond that'd take my friend a year later),
once in a while catching a glimpse of my bobber,
now here, now there. Shadows grew fat
and dropped from trees into the pond. Finally
it was dark, and I biked home.

My dad was drunk
and in the kitchen with a woman not his wife, nor
my mother either. This woman was, I swear, sitting
on his lap, drinking a beer. A woman
with part of a front tooth
missing. She tried to grin as she rose
to her feet. My dad stayed where he was, staring at me
as if he didn't recognize his own get. *Here,*
what is it boy? he said. *What happened,*
son? Swaying against the sink, the woman wet her lips
and waited for whatever was to happen next.
My dad waited too, there in his old place
at the kitchen table, the bulge in his pants
subsiding. We all waited and wondered
at the stuttered syllables, the words made to cling
as anguish that poured from my raw young mouth.

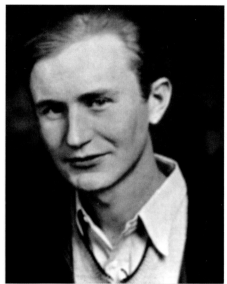
Family photo of Ray's father, Raymond Clevie Carver.

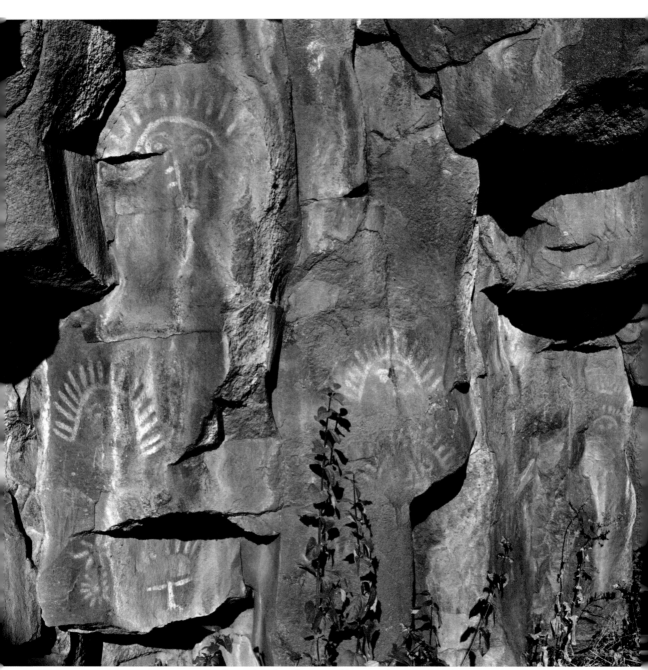

Indian Painted Rock, near Yakima, Washington. (1989)

From "Tell The Women We're Going"

He pulled off the road under some trees. The highway forked here at Picture Rock, one road going on to Yakima, the other heading for Naches, Enumclaw, the Chinook Pass, Seattle.

A hundred yards off the road was a high, sloping, black mound of rock, part of a low range of hills, honey-combed with footpaths and small caves, Indian sign-painting here and there on the cave walls. The cliff side of the rock faced the highway and all over it there were things like this: NACHES 67—GLEED WILDCATS—JESUS SAVES—BEAT YAKIMA—REPENT NOW.

From "Nobody Said Anything"

The fish wasn't in the run below the riffle, and we couldn't see him in the next stretch, either. We looked at each other and began to worry that the fish really had gone far enough downstream to reach one of the deep holes. But then the goddamn thing rolled near the bank, actually knocking dirt into the water with his tail and took off again. He went through another riffle, his big tail sticking out of the water. I saw him cruise over near the bank and stop, his tail half out of the water, finning just enough to hold against the current.

"Do you see him?" I said. The boy looked. I took his arm and pointed his finger. "Right *there*. Okay now, listen. I'll go down to that little run between those banks. See where I mean? You wait here until I give you a signal. Then you start down. Okay? And this time don't let him get by you if he heads back."

"Yeah," the boy said and worked his lip with those teeth. "Let's get him this time," the boy said, a terrible look of cold in his face.

I got up on the bank and walked down, making sure I moved quiet. I slid off the bank and waded in again. But I couldn't see the great big son of a bitch and my heart turned. I thought it might have taken off already. A little farther downstream and it would get to one of the holes. We would never get him then.

"He still there?" I hollered. I held my breath.

The kid waved.

"Ready!" I hollered again.

"Here goes!" the kid hollered back.

My hands shook. The creek was about three feet wide and ran between dirt banks. The water was low but fast. The kid was moving down the creek now, water up to his knees, throwing rocks ahead of him, splashing and shouting.

"Here he comes!" The kid waved his arms. I saw the fish now; it was coming right at me. He tried to turn when he saw me, but it was too late. I went down on my knees, grasping in the cold water. I scooped him with my hands and arms, up, up, raising him, throwing him out of the water, both of us falling onto the bank. I held him against my shirt, him flopping and twisting, until I could get my hands up his slippery sides to his gills. I ran one hand in and clawed through to his mouth and locked around his jaw. I knew I had him. He was still flopping and hard to hold, but I had him and I wasn't going to let go.

"We got him!" the boy hollered, as he splashed up. "We got him, by God! Ain't he something! Look at him! Oh God, let me hold him", the boy hollered.

"We got to kill him first," I said. I ran my other hand down the throat. I pulled back on the head as hard as I could, trying to watch out for the teeth, and felt the heavy crunching. He gave a long slow tremble and was still. I laid him on the bank and we looked at him. He was at least two feet long, queerly skinny, but bigger than anything I had ever caught. I took hold of his jaw again.

"Hey," the kid said but didn't say any more when he saw what I was going to do. I washed off the blood and laid the fish back on the bank.

"I want to show him to my dad so bad," the kid said. We were wet and shivering. We looked at him, kept touching him. We pried open his big mouth and felt his rows of teeth. His sides were scarred, whitish welts as big as quarters and kind of puffy. There were nicks out of his head around his eyes and on his snout where I guess he had banged into the rocks and been in fights. But he was so skinny, too skinny for how long he was, and you could hardly see the pink stripe down his sides, and his belly was gray and slack instead of white and solid like it should have been. But I thought he was something.

Overleaf: Bachelor Creek, near Yakima, Washington, the setting for "Nobody Said Anything." (1989)

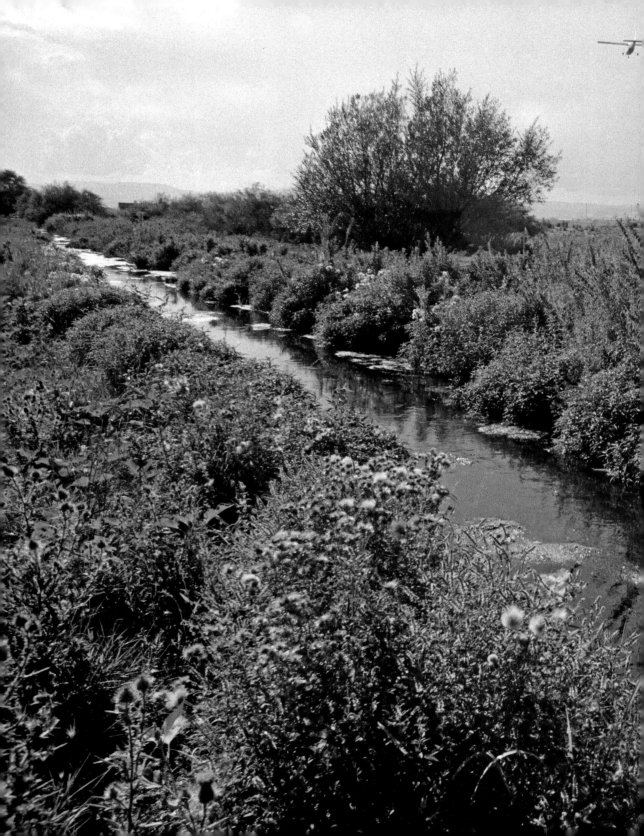

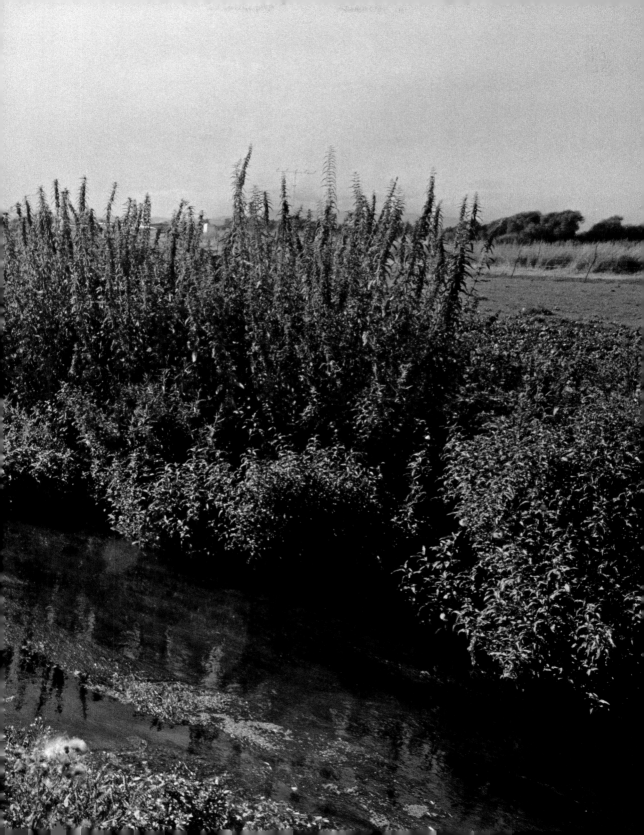

Wenas Ridge

The seasons turning. Memory flaring.
Three of us that fall. Young hoodlums—
shoplifters, stealers of hubcaps.
Bozos. Dick Miller, dead now.
Lyle Rousseau, son of the Ford dealer.
And I, who'd just made a girl pregnant.
Hunting late into that golden afternoon
for grouse. Following deer paths,
pushing through undergrowth, stepping over
blow-downs. Reaching out for something to hold onto.

At the top of Wenas Ridge
we walked out of pine trees and could see
down deep ravines, where the wind roared, to the river.
More alive then, I thought, than I'd ever be.
But my whole life, in switchbacks, ahead of me.

Hawks, deer, coons we looked at and let go.
Killed six grouse and should have stopped.
Didn't, though we had limits.

Lyle and I climbing fifty feet or so
above Dick Miller. Who screamed—"Yaaaah!"
Then swore and swore. Legs numbing as I saw what.
That fat, dark snake rising up. Beginning to sing.
And how it sang! A timber rattler thick as my wrist.
It'd struck at Miller, but missed. No other way
to say it—he was paralyzed. Could scream, and swear,

not shoot. Then the snake lowered itself from sight
and went in under rocks. We understood
we'd have to get down. In the same way we'd got up.
Blindly crawling through brush, stepping over blow-downs,
pushing into undergrowth. Shadows falling from trees now
onto flat rocks that held the day's heat. And snakes.
My heart stopped, and then started again.
My hair stood on end. This was the moment
my life had prepared me for. And I wasn't ready.

We started down anyway. Jesus, please help me
out of this, I prayed. I'll believe in you again
and honor you always. But Jesus was crowded out
of my head by the vision of that rearing snake.
That singing. Keep believing in me, snake said,
for I will return. I made an obscure, criminal pact
that day. Praying to Jesus in one breath.
To snake in the other. Snake finally more real
to me. The memory of that day
like a blow to the calf now.

I got out, didn't I? But something happened.
I married the girl I loved, yet poisoned her life.
Lies began to coil in my heart and call it home.
Got used to darkness and its crooked ways.
Since then I've always feared rattlesnakes.
Been ambivalent about Jesus.
But someone, something's responsible for this.
Now, as then.

Overleaf: Wenas Ridge, Washington. (1989)

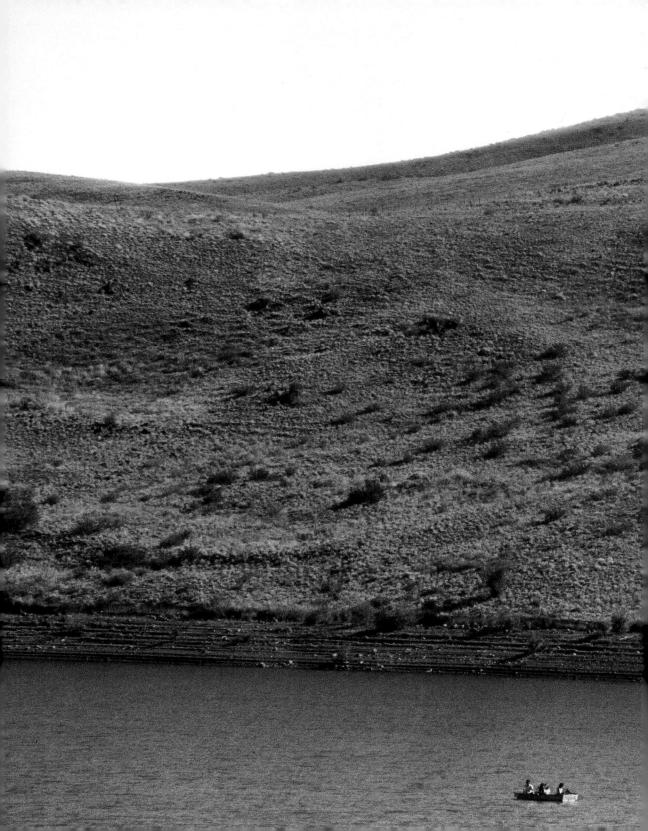

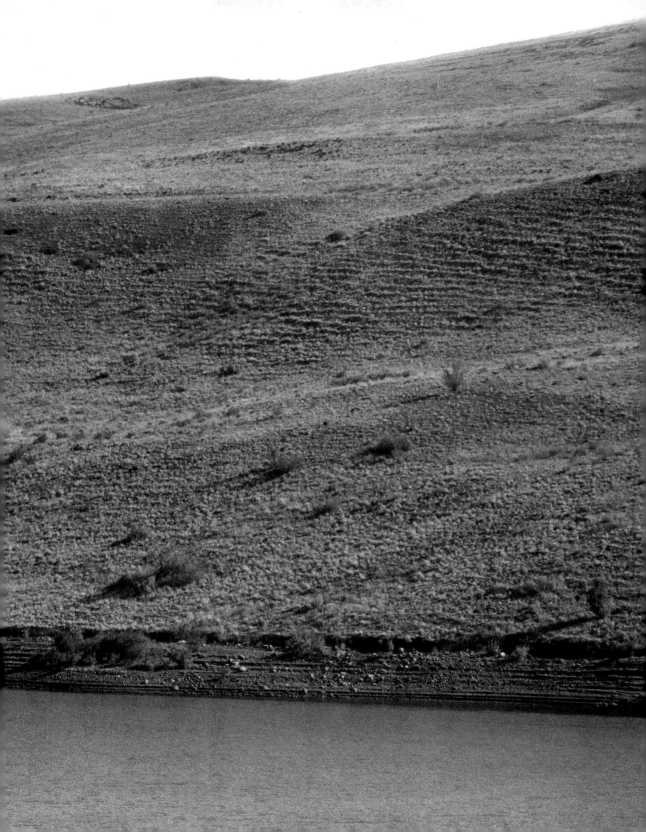

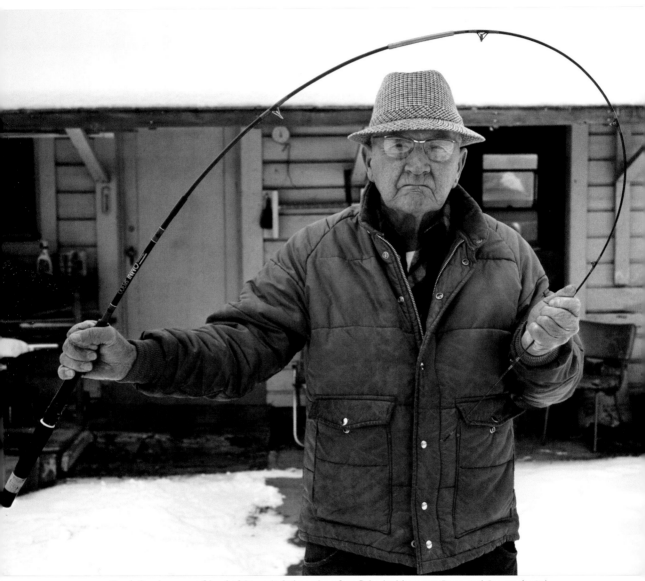

Frank Sandmeyer, a friend of Carver's father who often fished with young Raymond Carver. (1989)

From "Distance"

The boy liked Carl Sutherland. He'd been a friend of the boy's father, who was dead now. After the father's death, maybe trying to replace a loss they both felt, the boy and Sutherland had started hunting together. Sutherland was a lean, balding man who lived alone and was not given to casual talk. Once in a while, when they were together, the boy felt uncomfortable, wondered if he had said or done something wrong because he was not used to being around people who kept still for long periods of time. But when he did talk the older man was often opinionated, and frequently the boy didn't agree with the opinions. Yet the man had a toughness and woods-savvy about him that the boy liked and admired.

From "Distance"

Sally was the girl's sister. She was ten years older. The boy was a little in love with her just as he was a little in love with Betsy, who was another sister the girl had. He'd said to the girl, if we weren't married I could go for Sally.

What about Betsy? the girl had said. I hate to admit it but I truly feel she's better looking than Sally or me. What about her?

Betsy too, the boy said and laughed. But not in the same way I could go for Sally. There's something about Sally you could fall for. No, I believe I'd prefer Sally over Betsy, if I had to make a choice.

But who do you really love? the girl asked. Who do you love most in all the world? Who's your wife?

You're my wife, the boy said.

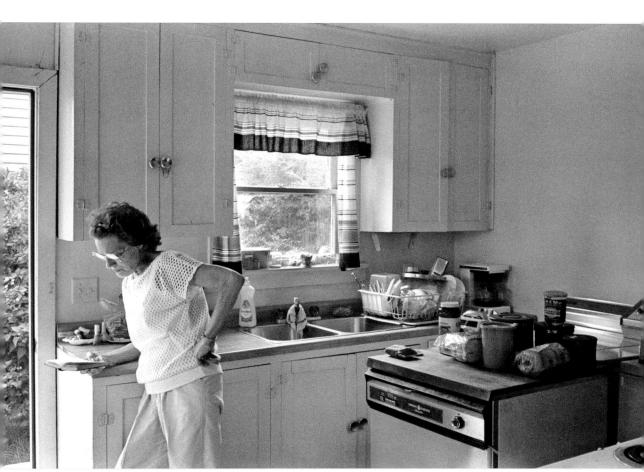

Jerry Davis, Maryann Carver's older sister, Yakima, Washington. (1989)

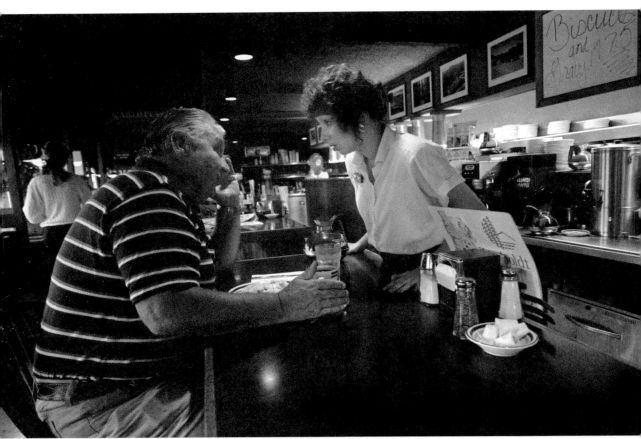

The Humboldt Diner, Arcata, California. (1989)

From "They're Not Your Husband"

Earl Ober was between jobs as a salesman. But Doreen, his wife, had gone to work nights as a waitress at a twenty-four-hour coffee shop at the edge of town. One night, when he was drinking, Earl decided to stop by the coffee shop and have something to eat. He wanted to see where Doreen worked, and he wanted to see if he could order something on the house.

He sat at the counter and studied the menu.

"What are you doing here?" Doreen said when she saw him sitting there.

She handed over an order to the cook. "What are you going to order, Earl?" she said. "The kids okay?"

"They're fine," Earl said. "I'll have coffee and one of those Number Two sandwiches."

Doreen wrote it down.

"Any chance of, you know?" he said to her and winked.

"No," she said. "Don't talk to me now. I'm busy."

Earl drank his coffee and waited for the sandwich. Two men in business suits, their ties undone, their collars open, sat down next to him and asked for coffee. As Doreen walked away with the coffeepot, one of the men said to the other, "Look at the ass on that. I don't believe it."

The other man laughed. "I've seen better," he said.

"That's what I mean," the first man said. "But some jokers like their quim fat."

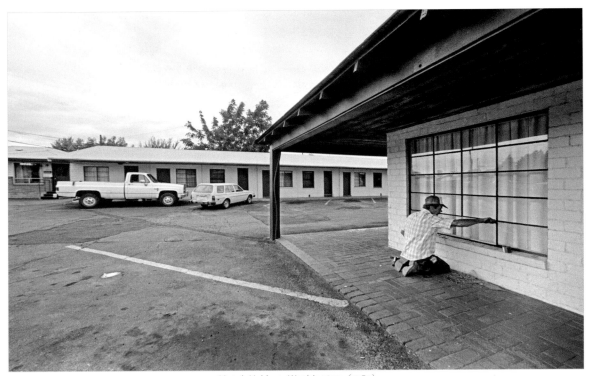

Motel, Yakima, Washington. (1989)

From "Gazebo"

That morning she pours Teacher's over my belly and licks it off. That afternoon she tries to jump out the window.

I go, "Holly, this can't continue. This has got to stop."

We are sitting on the sofa in one of the upstairs suites. There were any number of vacancies to choose from. But we needed a suite, a place to move around in and be able to talk. So we'd locked up the motel office that morning and gone upstairs to a suite. . . .

When we'd first moved down here and taken over as managers, we thought we were out of the woods. Free rent and free utilities plus three hundred a month. You couldn't beat it with a stick.

Holly took care of the books. She was good with figures, and she did most of the renting of the units. She liked people, and people liked her back. I saw to the grounds, mowed the grass and cut weeds, kept the swimming pool clean, did the small repairs.

Everything was fine for the first year. I was holding down another job nights, and we were getting ahead. We had plans. Then one morning, I don't know. I'd just laid some bathroom tile in one of the units when this little Mexican maid comes in to clean. It was Holly had hired her. I can't really say I'd noticed the little thing before, though we spoke when we saw each other. She called me, I remember, Mister.

Anyway, one thing and the other.

So after that morning I started paying attention. She was a neat little thing with fine white teeth. I used to watch her mouth.

She started calling me by my name.

One morning I was doing a washer for one of the bathroom faucets, and she comes in and turns on the TV as maids are like to do. While they clean, that is. I stopped what I was doing and stepped outside the bathroom. She was surprised to see me. She smiles and says my name.

It was right after she said it that we got down on the bed....

"When we were just kids before we married?" Holly goes. "When we had big plans and hopes? You remember?" She was sitting on the bed, holding her knees and her drink.

"I remember, Holly."

"You weren't my first you know. My first was Wyatt. Imagine. Wyatt. And your name's Duane. Wyatt and Duane. Who knows what I was missing all those years? You were my everything, just like the song."

I go, "You're a wonderful woman, Holly. I know you've had the opportunities."

"But I didn't take them up on it!" she goes. "I couldn't go outside the marriage."

"Holly, please," I go. "No more now, honey. Let's not torture ourselves. What is it we should do?"

"Listen," she goes. "You remember the time we drove out to that old farm place outside of Yakima, out past Terrace Heights? We were just driving around? We were on this little dirt road and it was hot and dusty? We kept going and came to that old house, and you asked

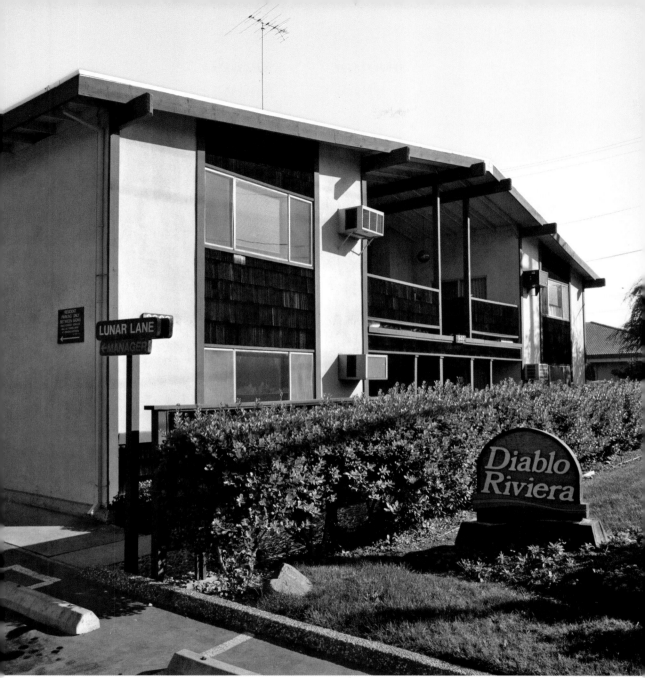

The apartment complex in Sacramento, California, that was the reference for "Gazebo." (1989)

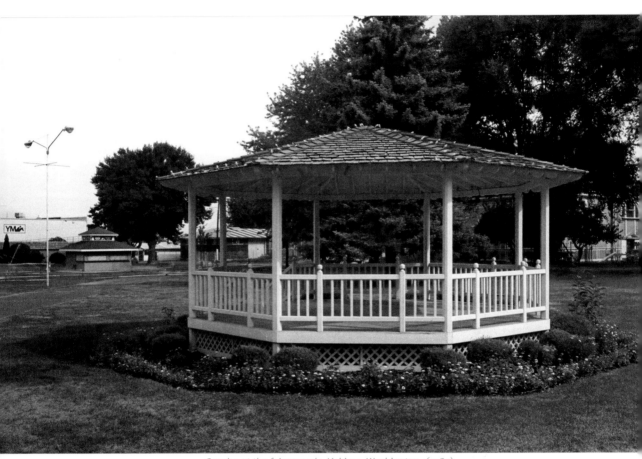

Gazebo at the fairgrounds, Yakima, Washington. (1989)

if we could have a drink of water? Can you imagine us doing that now? Going up to a house and asking for a drink of water?

"Those old people must be dead now," she goes, "side by side out there in some cemetery. You remember they asked us in for cake? And later on they showed us around? And there was this gazebo there out back? It was out back under some trees? It had a little peaked roof and the paint was gone and there were these weeds growing up over the steps. And the woman said that years before, I mean a real long time ago, men used to come around and play music out there on a Sunday, and the people would sit and listen. I thought we'd be like that too when we got old enough. Dignified. And in a place. And people would come to our door."

I can't say anything just yet. Then I go, "Holly, these things, we'll look back on them too. We'll go, 'Remember the motel with all the crud in the pool?'" I go, "You see what I'm saying, Holly?"

But Holly just sits there on the bed with her glass.

I can see she doesn't know.

I move over to the window and look out from behind the curtain. Someone says something below and rattles the door to the office. I stay there. I pray for a sign from Holly. I pray for Holly to show me.

I hear a car start. Then another. They turn on their lights against the building and, one after the other, they pull away and go out into the traffic.

"Duane," Holly goes.

In this too, she was right.

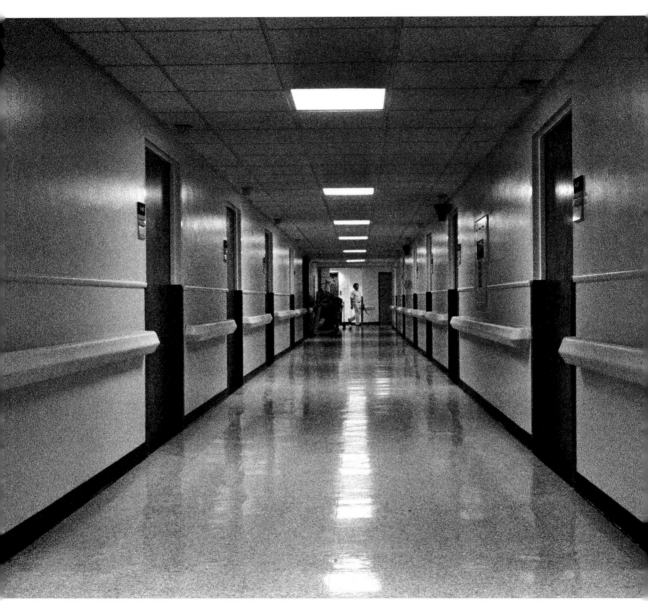

Mercy Hospital in Sacramento, California, where Carver worked nights. (1989)

From "Vitamins"

I had a job and Patti didn't. I worked a few hours a night for the hospital. It was a nothing job. I did some work, signed the card for eight hours, went drinking with the nurses. After a while, Patti wanted a job. She said she needed a job for her self-respect. So she started selling multiple vitamins door to door.

For a while she was just another girl who went up and down blocks in strange neighborhoods, knocking on doors. But she learned the ropes. She was quick and had excelled at things in school. She had personality. Pretty soon the company gave her a promotion. Some of the girls who weren't doing so hot were put to work under her. Before long, she had herself a crew and a little office out in the mall. But the girls who worked for her were always changing. Some would quit after a couple of days—after a couple of hours, sometimes. But sometimes there were girls who were good at it. They could sell vitamins. These were the girls that stuck with Patti. They formed the core of the crew. But there were girls who couldn't give away vitamins.

The girls who couldn't cut it would quit. Just not show up for work. If they had a phone, they'd take it off the hook. They wouldn't answer the door. Patti took these losses to heart, like the girls were new converts who had lost their way. She blamed herself. But she got over it. There were too many not to get over it.

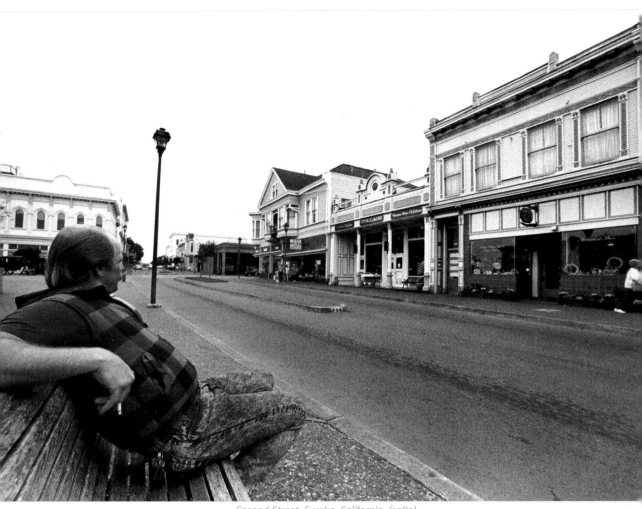

Second Street, Eureka, California. (1989)

From "Will You Please Be Quiet, Please?"

He came to Second Street, the part of town people called "Two Street." It started here at Shelton, under the street light where the old rooming houses ended, and ran for four or five blocks on down to the pier, where fishing boats tied up. He had been down here once, six years ago, to a secondhand shop to finger through the dusty shelves of old books. There was a liquor store across the street, and he could see a man standing just inside the glass door, looking at a newspaper.

A bell over the door tinkled. Ralph almost wept from the sound of it. He bought some cigarettes and went out again, continuing along the street, looking in windows, some with signs taped up: a dance, the Shrine circus that had come and gone last summer, an election—*Fred C. Walters for Councilman.* One of the windows he looked through had sinks and pipe joints scattered around on a table, and this too brought tears to his eyes. He came to a Vic Tanney gym where he could see light sneaking under the curtains pulled across a big window and could hear water splashing in the pool inside and the echo of exhilarated voices calling across water. There was more fight now, coming from bars and cafes on both sides of the street, and more people, groups of three or four, but now and then a man by himself or a woman in bright slacks walking rapidly. He stopped in front of a window and watched some Negroes shooting pool, smoke drifting in the light burning above the table. One of the men, chalking his cue, hat on, cigarette in his mouth, said something to another man and both men grinned, and then the first man looked intently at the balls and lowered himself over the table.

Ralph stopped in front of Jim's Oyster House. He had never been here before, had never been to any of these places before. Above the door the name was spelled out in yellow lightbulbs: JIM'S OYSTER HOUSE. Above this, fixed to an iron grill there was a huge neon-lighted clam shell with a man's legs sticking out. The torso was hidden in the shell and the legs flashed red, on and off, up and down, so that they seemed to be kicking. Ralph lit another cigarette from the one he had and pushed the door open. It was crowded, people bunched on the dance floor, their arms laced around each other, waiting in positions for the band to begin again. Ralph pushed his way to the bar, and once a drunken woman took hold of his coat. There were no stools and he had to stand at the end of the bar between a Coast Guardsman and a shriveled man in denims. In the mirror he could see the men in the band getting up from the table where they had been sitting. They wore white shirts and dark slacks with little red string ties around their necks. There was a fireplace with gas flames behind a stack of metal logs, and the band platform was to the side of this. One of the musicians plucked the strings of his electric guitar, said some thing to the others with a knowing grin. The band began to play.

Ralph raised his glass and drained it. Down the bar he could hear a woman say angrily, "Well, there's going to be trouble, that's all I've got to say." The musicians came to the end of their number and started another. One of the men, the bass player, moved to the microphone and began to sing. But Ralph could not understand the words. When the band took another break, Ralph looked around

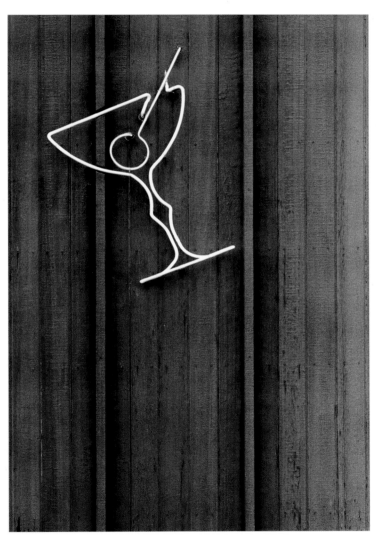

Facade of a bar with a neon sign, Arcata, California. (1989)

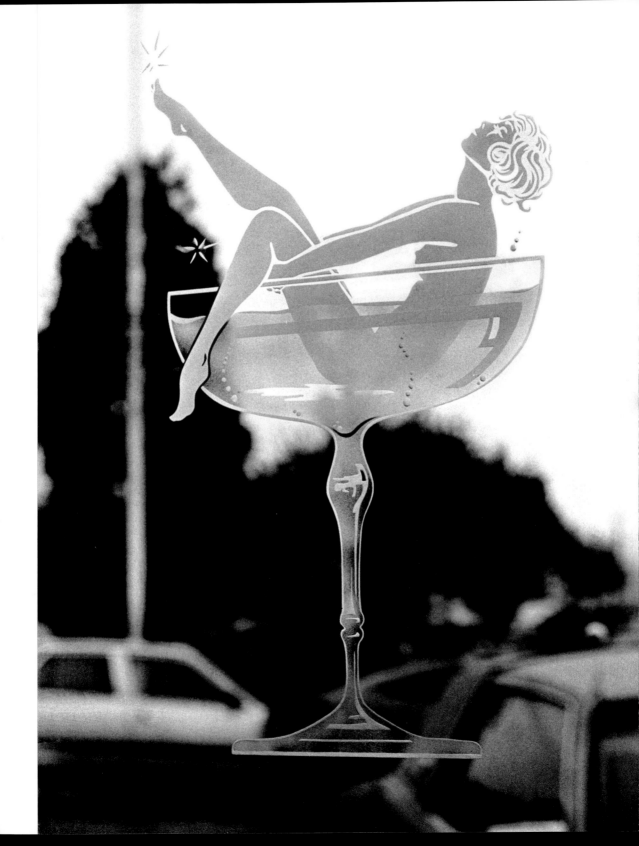

for the toilet. He could make out doors opening and closing at the far end of the bar and headed in that direction. He staggered a little and knew he was drunk now. Over one of the doors was a rack of antlers. He saw a man go in and he saw another man catch the door and come out. Inside, in line behind three other men, he found himself staring at opened thighs and vulva drawn on the wall over a pocket-comb machine. Beneath was scrawled EAT ME, and lower down someone had added *Betty M. Eats It— RA 52275*. The man ahead moved up, and Ralph took a step forward, his heart squeezed in the weight of Betty. Finally, he moved to the bowl and urinated. It was a bolt of lightning, cracking. He sighed, leaned forward, and let his head rest against the wall. Oh, Betty, he thought. His life had changed, he was willing to understand. Were there other men, he wondered drunkenly, who could look at one event in their lives and perceive in it the tiny makings of the catastrophe that thereafter set their lives on a different course? He stood there a while longer, and then he looked down: he had urinated on his fingers. He moved to the wash basin, ran water over his hands after deciding against the dirty bar of soap. As he was unrolling the towel, he put his face up close to the pitted mirror and looked into his eyes. A face: nothing out of the ordinary. He touched the glass, and then he moved away as a man tried to get past him to the sink.

Bar window, Arcata, California. (1989)

Overleaf: Bar, Arcata, California. (1989)

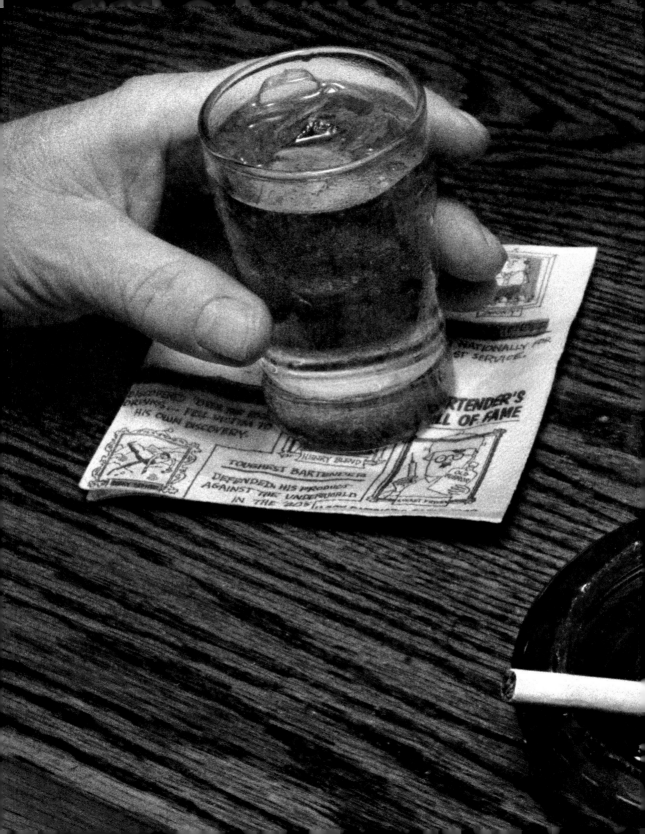

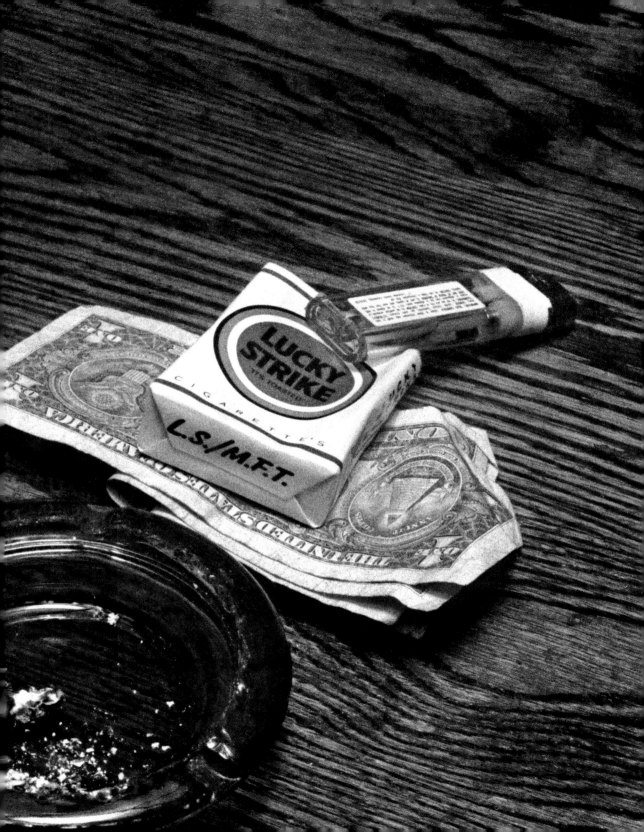

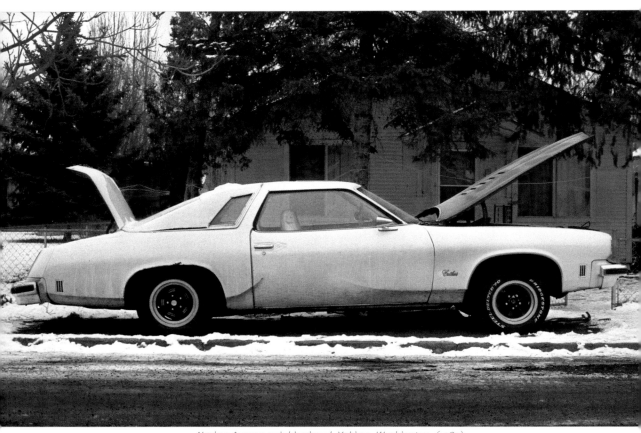

Naches Avenue neighborhood, Yakima, Washington. (1987)

The Car

The car with a cracked windshield.
The car that threw a rod.
The car without brakes.
The car with a faulty U-joint.
The car with a hole in its radiator.
The car I picked peaches for.
The car with a cracked block.
The car with no reverse gear.
The car I traded for a bicycle.
The car with steering problems.
The car with generator trouble.
The car with no back seat.
The car with the torn front seat.
The car that burned oil.
The car with rotten hoses.
The car that left the restaurant without paying.
The car with bald tires.
The car with no heater or defroster.
The car with its front end out of alignment.
The car the child threw up in.
The car I threw up in.
The car with the broken water pump.
The car whose timing gear was shot.
The car with a blown head-gasket.
The car I left on the side of the road.
The car that leaked carbon monoxide.
The car with a sticky carburetor.

The car that hit the dog and kept going.
The car with a hole in its muffler.
The car with no muffler.
The car my daughter wrecked.
The car with the twice-rebuilt engine.
The car with corroded battery cables.
The car bought with a bad check.
Car of my sleepless nights.
The car with a stuck thermostat.
The car whose engine caught fire.
The car with no headlights.
The car with a broken fan belt.
The car with wipers that wouldn't work.
The car I gave away.
The car with transmission trouble.
The car I washed my hands of.
The car I struck with a hammer.
The car with payments that couldn't be met.
The repossessed car.
The car whose clutch-pin broke.
The car waiting on the back lot.
Car of my dreams.
My car.

Bankruptcy

Twenty-eight, hairy belly hanging out
of my undershirt (exempt)
I lie here on my side
on the couch (exempt)
and listen to the strange sound
of my wife's pleasant voice (also exempt).

We are new arrivals
to these small pleasures.
Forgive me (I pray the Court)
that we have been improvident.
Today, my heart, like the front door,
stands open for the first time in months.

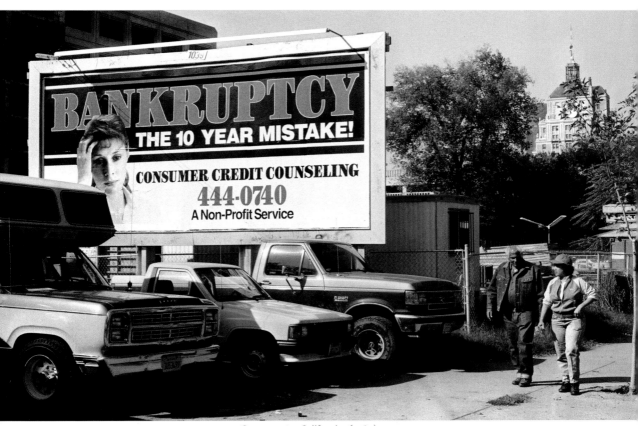

Sacramento, California. (1989)

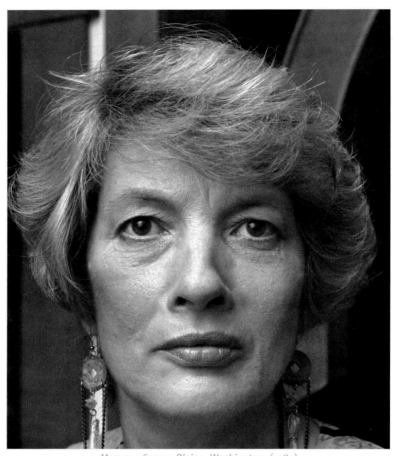

Maryann Carver, Blaine, Washington. (1989)

Miracle

They're on a one-way flight, bound from LAX
to SFO, both of them drunk and strung-out
having just squirmed through the hearing,
their second bankruptcy in seven years.
And who knows what, if anything, was said
on the plane, or who said it?
It could have been accumulation
of the day's events, or years on years
of failure and corruption that triggered violence.

Earlier, turned inside out, crucified and left
for dead, they'd been dropped like so much
garbage in front of the terminal. But
once inside they found their bearings,
took refuge in an airport lounge where they tossed
back doubles under a banner that read *Go Dodgers!*
They were plastered, as usual, as they buckled
into their seats and, as always, ready to assume
it was the universal human condition, this battle
waged continually with forces past all reckoning,
forces beyond mere human understanding.
But she's cracking. She can't take any more
and soon, without a word, she turns
in her seat and drills him. Punches him and
punches him, and he takes it.

Knowing deep down he deserves it ten times over—
whatever she wants to dish out—he is being
deservedly beaten for something, there are
good reasons. All the while his head is pummeled,
buffeted back and forth, her fists falling
against his ear, his lips, his jaw, he protects
his whiskey. Grips that plastic glass as if, yes,
it's the long-sought treasure right there
on the tray in front of him.

She keeps on until his nose begins to bleed
and it's then he asks her to stop. *Please, baby,
for Christ's sake, stop.* It may be his plea
reaches her as a faint signal from another
galaxy, a dying star, for this is what it is,
a coded sign from some other time and place
needling her brain, reminding her of something
so lost it's gone forever. In any event, she stops
hitting him, goes back to her drink. Why
does she stop? Because she remembers
the fat years preceding the lean? All that history
they'd shared, sticking it out together, the two
of them against the world? No way. If she'd truly
remembered everything and those years had dropped
smack into her lap all at once,
she would've killed him on the spot.

Maybe her arms are tired, that's why she stops.
Say she's tired then. So she stops. He picks up
his drink almost as if nothing's happened
though it has, of course, and his head aches
and reels with it. She goes back to her whiskey
without a word, not even so much as the usual

"bastard" or "son of a bitch." Dead quiet.
He's silent as lice. Holds the drink
napkin under his nose to catch the blood,
turns his head slowly to look out.

Far below, the small steady lights in houses
up and down some coastal valley. It's
the dinner hour down there. People pushing
up to a full table, grace being said,
hands joined together under roofs so solid
they will never blow off those houses—houses where,
he imagines, decent people live and eat, pray
and pull together. People who, if they left
their tables and looked up from the dining
room windows, could see a harvest moon and,
just below, like a lighted insect, the dim glow
of a jet liner. He strains to see over
the wing and beyond, to the myriad lights
of the city they are rapidly approaching,
the place where they live with others of their kind,
the place they call home.

He looks around the cabin. Other people,
that's all. People like themselves
in a way, male or female, one sex
or the other, people not entirely unlike
themselves—hair, ears, eyes, nose, shoulders,
genitals—my God, even the clothes they wear
are similar, and there's that identifying strap
around the middle. But he knows he and she
are not like those others though he'd like it,
and she too, if they were.

Blood soaks his napkin. His head rings and rings
but he can't answer it. And what would he say
if he could? *I'm sorry they're not in. They left
here, and there too, years ago.* They tear
through the thin night air, belted in, bloody husband
and wife, both so still and pale they could be
dead. But they're not, and that's part of
the miracle. All this is one more giant step
into the mysterious experience of their lives.
Who could have foretold any of it years back when,
their hands guiding the knife, they made
that first cut deep into the wedding cake?
Then the next. Who would have listened?
Anyone bringing such tidings of the future
would have been scourged from the gate.

The plane lifts, then banks sharply. He touches
her arm. She lets him. She even takes his hand.
They were made for each other, right? It's fate.
They'll survive. They'll land and pull themselves
together, walk away from this awful fix—
they simply have to, they must.
There's lots in store for them yet, so many fierce
surprises, such exquisite turnings. It's now
they have to account for, the blood
on his collar, the dark smudge of it
staining her cuff.

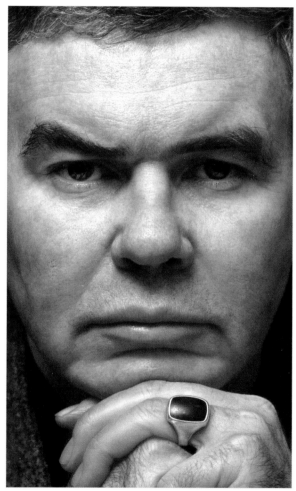

Raymond Carver, Port Angeles, Washington. (1987)

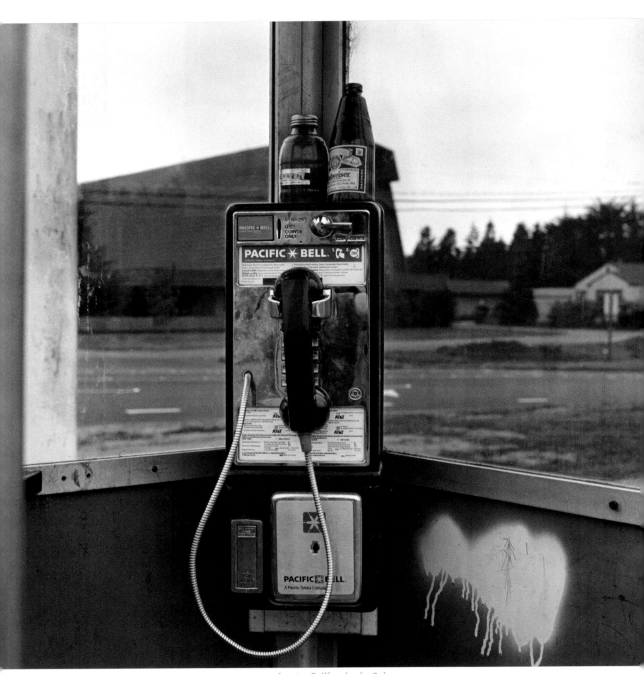

Arcata, California. (1989)

The Phone Booth

She slumps in the booth, weeping
into the phone. Asking a question
or two, and weeping some more.
Her companion, an old fellow in jeans
and denim shirt, stands waiting
his turn to talk, and weep.
She hands him the phone.
For a minute they are together
in the tiny booth, his tears
dropping alongside hers. Then
she goes to lean against the fender
of their sedan. And listens
to him talk about arrangements.

I watch all this from my car.
I don't have a phone at home, either.
I sit behind the wheel,
smoking, waiting to make
my own arrangements. Pretty soon
he hangs up. Comes out and wipes his face.
They get in the car and sit
with the windows rolled up.
The glass grows steamy as she
leans into him, as he puts
his arm around her shoulders.
The workings of comfort in that
              cramped, public place.

I take my small change over
to the booth, and step inside.
But leaving the door open, it's
so close in there. The phone still
              warm to the touch.

I hate to use a phone
that's just brought news of death.
But I have to, it being the only phone
for miles, and one that might
listen without taking sides.

I put in coins and wait.
Those people in the car wait too.
He starts the engine then kills it.
Where to? None of us able
to figure it. Not knowing
where the next blow might fall,
or why. The ringing at the other end
stops when she picks it up.
Before I can say two words, the phone
begins to shout, "I told you it's over!
Finished! You can go
to hell as far as I'm concerned!"

I drop the phone and pass my hand
across my face. I close and open the door.
The couple in the sedan roll
their windows down and
watch, their tears stilled
for a moment in the face of this distraction.
Then they roll their windows up
and sit behind the glass. We
don't go anywhere for a while.
And then we go.

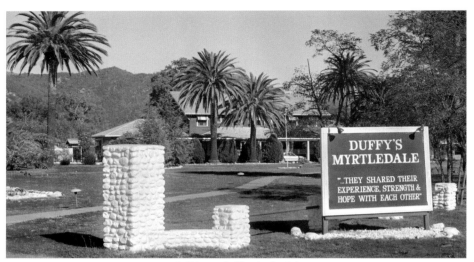

Calistoga, California. (1989)

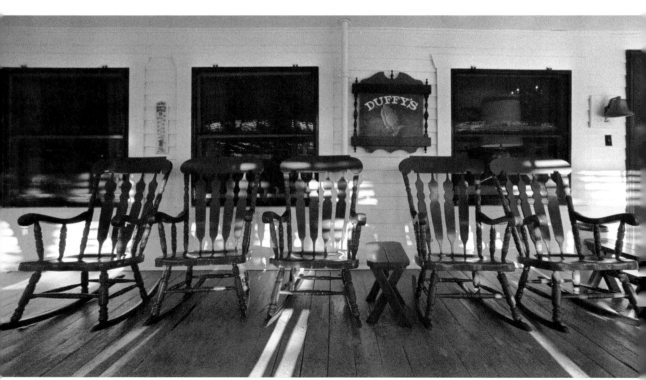

The front porch at Duffy's, Calistoga, California. (1989)

From "Where I'm Calling From"

J.P. and I are on the front porch at Frank Martin's drying-out facility. Like the rest of us at Frank Martin's, J.P. is first and foremost a drunk. But he's also a chimney sweep. It's his first time here, and he's scared. I've been here once before. What's to say? I'm back. J.P.'s real name is Joe Penny, but he says I should call him J.P. He's about thirty years old. Younger than I am. Not much younger, but a little. He's telling me how he decided to go into his line of work, and he wants to use his hands when he talks. But his hands tremble. I mean, they won't keep still. "This has never happened to me before," he says. He means the trembling. I tell him I sympathize. I tell him the shakes will idle down. And they will. But it takes time.

We've only been in here a couple of days. We're not out of the woods yet. J.P. has these shakes, and every so often a nerve—maybe it isn't a nerve, but it's something—begins to jerk in my shoulder. Sometimes it's at the side of my neck. When this happens, my mouth dries up. It's an effort just to swallow then. I know something's about to happen and I want to head it off. I want to hide from it, that's what I want to do. Just close my eyes and let it pass by, let it take the next man. J.P. can wait a minute. . . .

"Keep talking, J.P. Then what?" I say.

When he was eighteen or nineteen years old and out of high school and had nothing whatsoever he wanted to do with his life, he went across town one afternoon to visit a friend. This friend lived in a house with a fireplace. J.P. and his friend sat around drinking beer and batting the breeze. They played some records. Then the doorbell rings. The friend goes to the door. This young woman chimney sweep is there with her cleaning things. She's wearing a top hat, the sight of which knocked J.P. for a loop. She tells J.P.'s friend that she has an appointment to clean the fireplace. The friend lets her in and bows. The young woman doesn't pay him any mind. She spreads a blanket on the hearth and lays out her gear. She's wearing these black pants, black shirt, black shoes and socks. Of course, by now she's taken her hat off. J.P. says it nearly drove him nuts to look at her. She does the work, she cleans the chimney, while J.P. and his friend play records and drink beer. But they watch her and they watch what she does. Now and then J.P. and his friend look at each other and grin or else they wink. They raise their eyebrows when the upper half of the young woman disappears into the chimney. She was all-right-looking, too, J.P. said.

When she'd finished her work, she rolled her things up in the blanket. From J.P.'s friend, she took a check that had been made out to her by his parents. And then she asks the friend if he wants to kiss her. "It's supposed to bring good luck," she says. That does it for J.P. The friend rolls his eyes. He clowns some more. Then, probably blushing, he kisses her on the cheek. At this minute, J.P. made his mind up about something. He put his beer down. He got up from the sofa. He went over to the young woman as she was starting to go out the door.

"Me, too?" J.P. said to her.

She swept her eyes over him. J.P. says he could feel his heart knocking. The young woman's name, it turns out, was Roxy.

"Sure," Roxy says. "Why not? I've got some extra kisses." And she kissed him a good one right on the lips and then turned to go. . . .

Roxy starts going out with him on dates. And little by little he talks her into letting him go along on jobs with her. But Roxy's in business with her father and brother and they've got just the right amount of work. They don't need anybody else. Besides, who was this guy J.P.? J.P. what? Watch out, they warned her.

So she and J.P. saw some movies together. They went to a few dances. But mainly the courtship revolved around their cleaning chimneys together. Before you know it, J.P. says, they're talking about tying the knot. And after a while they do it, they get married. J.P.'s new father-in-law takes him in as a full partner. In a year or so, Roxy has a kid. She's quit being a chimney sweep. At any rate, she's quit doing the work. Pretty soon she has another kid. J.P.'s in his mid-twenties by how. He's buying a house. He says he was happy with his life. "I was happy with the way things were going," he says. "I had

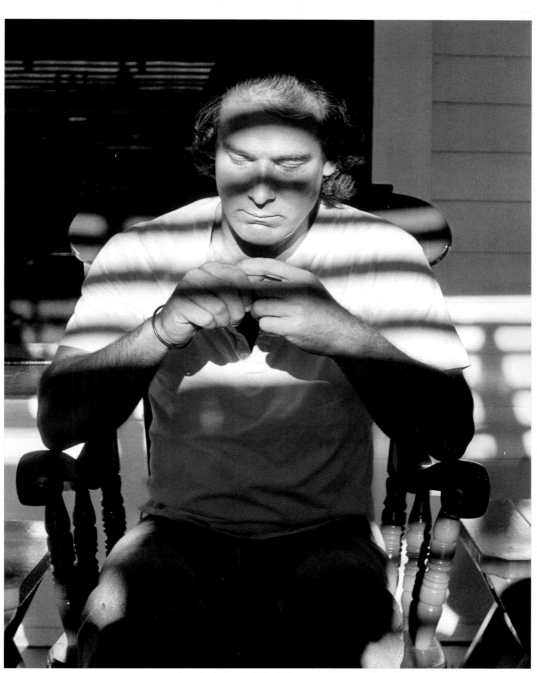

A recovering alcoholic, Duffy's, Calistoga, California. (1989)

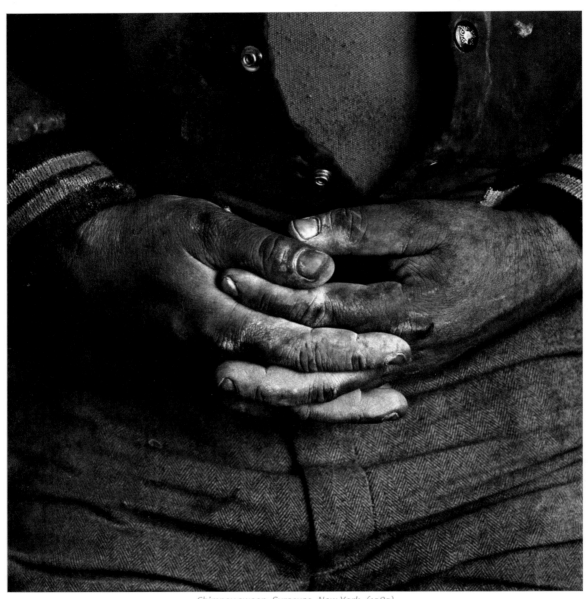

Chimney sweep, Syracuse, New York. (1989)

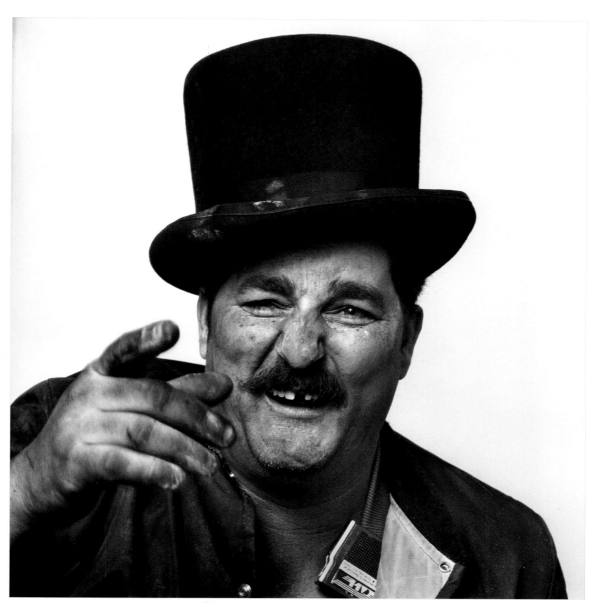

Chimney sweep, Syracuse, New York. (1989)

everything I wanted. I had a wife and kids I loved, and I was doing what I wanted to do with my life." But for some reason—who knows why we do what we do?—his drinking picks up. For a long time he drinks beer and beer only. Any kind of beer—it didn't matter. He says he could drink beer twenty-four hours a day. He'd drink beer at night while he watched TV. Sure, once in a while he drank hard stuff. But that was only if they went out on the town, which was not often, or else when they had company over. Then a time comes, he doesn't know why, when he makes the switch from beer to gin-and-tonic. And he'd have more gin-and-tonic after dinner, sitting in front of the TV. There was always a glass of gin-and-tonic in his hand. He says he actually liked the taste of it. He began stopping off after work for drinks before he went home to have more drinks. Then he began missing some dinners. He just wouldn't show up. Or else he'd show up, but he wouldn't want anything to eat. He'd filled up on snacks at the bar. Sometimes he'd walk in the door and for no good reason throw his lunch pail across the living room. When Roxy yelled at him, he'd turn around and go out again. He moved his drinking time up to early afternoon, while he was still supposed to be working. He tells me that he was starting off the morning with a couple of drinks. He'd have a belt of the stuff before he brushed his teeth. Then he'd have his coffee. He'd go to work with a thermos bottle of vodka in his lunch pail.

Inspirational reading, Duffy's, Calistoga, California. (1989)

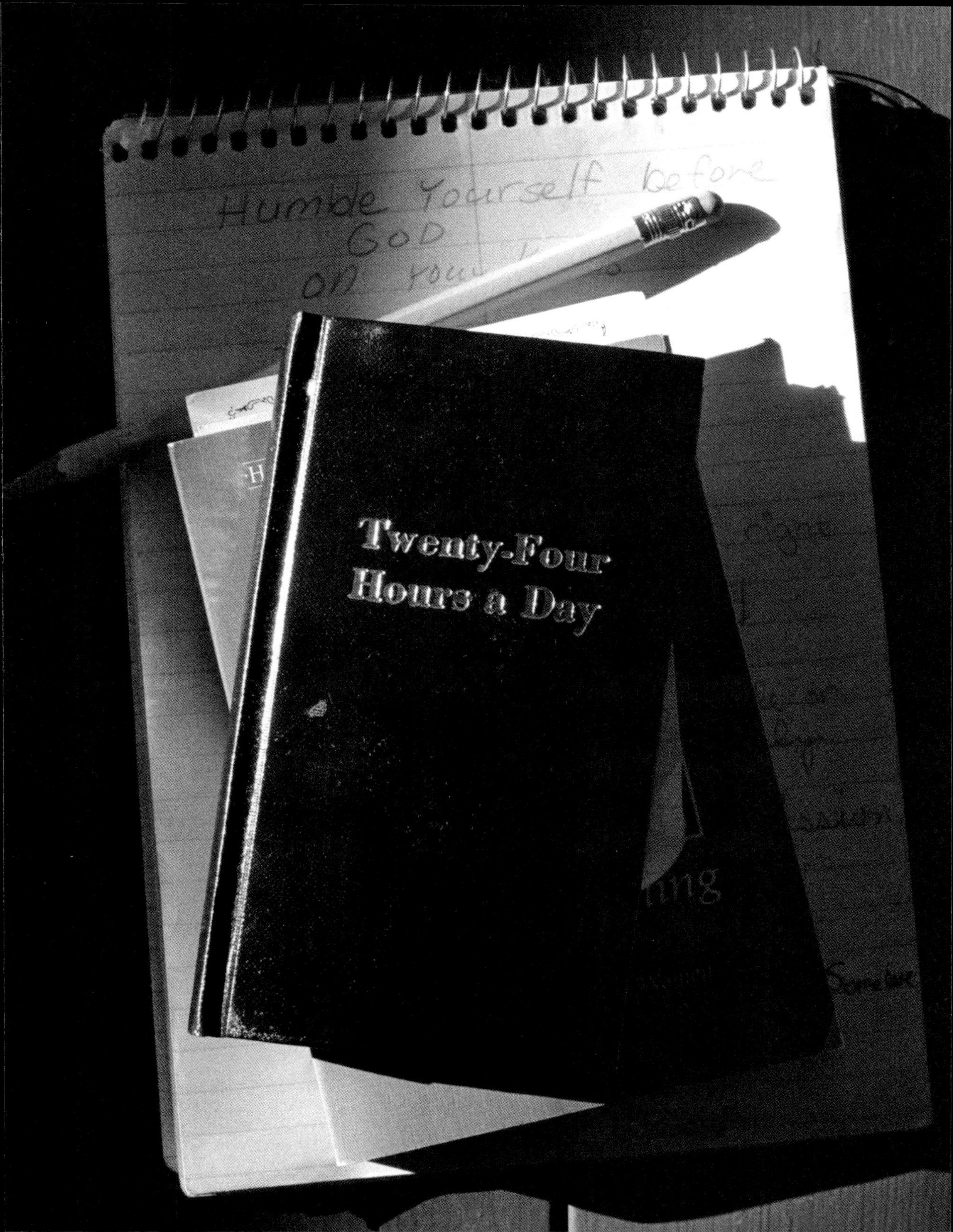
Humble Yourself before
GOD
Twenty-Four
Hours a Day

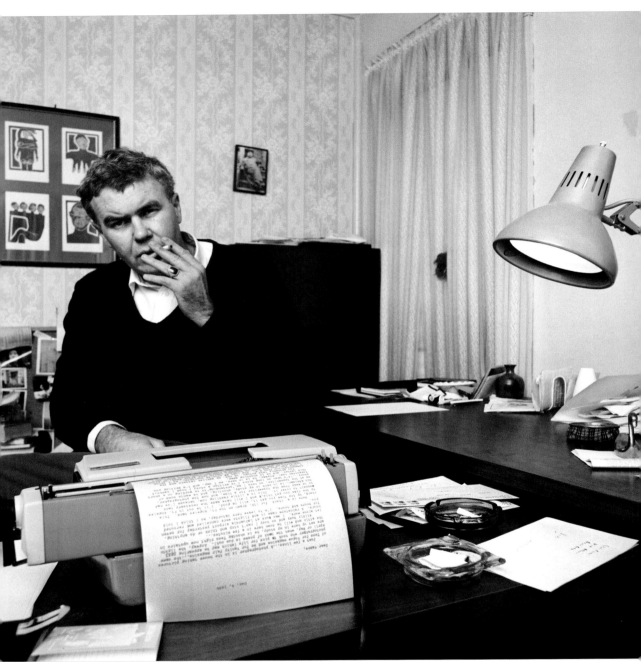

Raymond Carver, Syracuse, New York. (1984)

Dear Mr. Hallstrom

Thanks for your good letter. I was away from here for a few days
or else you would have had a reply from me before now.

Well, as you say, everyone's recovery is different, but it took
me at least six months—more—after I stopped drinking before I
could attempt to do any more than write a few letters. Mainly I was
so grateful to have my health back, and my life back, that it really
didn't matter to me in one large way if I ever wrote anything again,
or not. I wrote just a little bit, a story or two, if that, between six
months and eight or ten months after getting sober. Again, I must
say I didn't worry about it, in the largest sense. I remember feeling
that it was quite possible that I might never write anything "creative"
again, and that was all right, too, somehow. Finally, my letter writing
paid off, and I landed a one-year job teaching at the U of Texas at El
Paso. This would have been for the academic year 1978-1979. Fact,
I'd been sober for well over a year and I still wasn't writing, but I tell
you, and it's true, I wasn't worrying about it. I was just very happy,
very happy to be alive. Then, in El Paso, I wrote a few poems and
began to do a few book reviews (I was asked to do them and I was
pleased to be able to do them) for the *Chicago Tribune.* I don't think
I began to write seriously until the fall of 1979, when Tess and I were
living in Tucson, where she was teaching at the time (I'd somehow
been given a Guggenheim Fellowship, and I had that, and a job to

look forward to at Syracuse); and pretty soon that fall I started working on a story and finished it, and then began another one, and then another one. So, with the exception of a few book reviews, and a very few poems, after the first year of sobriety (and almost nothing the first year), it took me two years, a bit more than two years, to get into the swing of things again. I didn't know if I could do it again or not. It came, yes, but it came very, very slowly for the longest while after getting sober. Jesus, the whole drinking thing is such an ordeal and so much time and effort go into that, and your thinking is so fucked and your brains scrambled, it just takes the longest while to ever get on track again. But it'll come. Use this time of not writing to just get acquainted with yourself again, and do lots of reading and re-reading, the things that mattered so long ago when you were young and innocent, read those things over again. And go to AA meetings if it's necessary; and it was necessary for me for the longest while—six or eight months or so; and I've gone a number of times too since then, taking friends who wanted to go. But I don't think you should feel too anxious about the present situation. I mean, you just don't need any more than the usual anxiety right now, the anxieties we all walk around with, they're quite enough to deal with during this recovery period. Don't worry, try not to worry, about whether or not you will ever write again, or if you've wasted your life, or the better part of your life, by staying soused all the time. For the first month or so after getting sober, maybe two months, I felt absolutely crazy, nearly, every morning I woke up. I mean I felt great in one way, that I knew I was waking up sober, but I felt I'd pissed away years and years that

I'd never get back; and felt, too, like I hadn't done any work at all and that what I had done wasn't worth anything, etc. It's just that you're trying to put a life together, trying to make something out of just about nothing. It's starting over, and in a big way… And I wasn't able to write toward the end of my drinking career, either. I hardly wrote anything at all for the last two years of my drinking. So, add that to the long time it took me after getting sober, and you can see just where I was. Nowhere, but I was sober, and that was everything.

It'll come, you'll see. In its own good time, it'll come. Incidentally, I had a long conversation about this with the late Dick Hugo. He told me pretty much the same thing. The last years of his drinking, he was only writing one or two poems a year. And it took him a long while to get going again after he'd stopped.

Listen, I'm glad you wrote to me. I'm sorry if this seems hasty, or not very considered and thoughtful, but I wanted to get some kind of response back to you before any more time had elapsed.

Stay well. Don't drink, as they say. Think of me if ever you feel like you want to drink. I know if I can kick it, well, then there is hope for just about anybody. I had the world's worst case of it.

Write me again in a month or two, or whenever it's right, and tell me how you are and what you're doing.

This is with every good wish.

Warmly,

Ray Carver

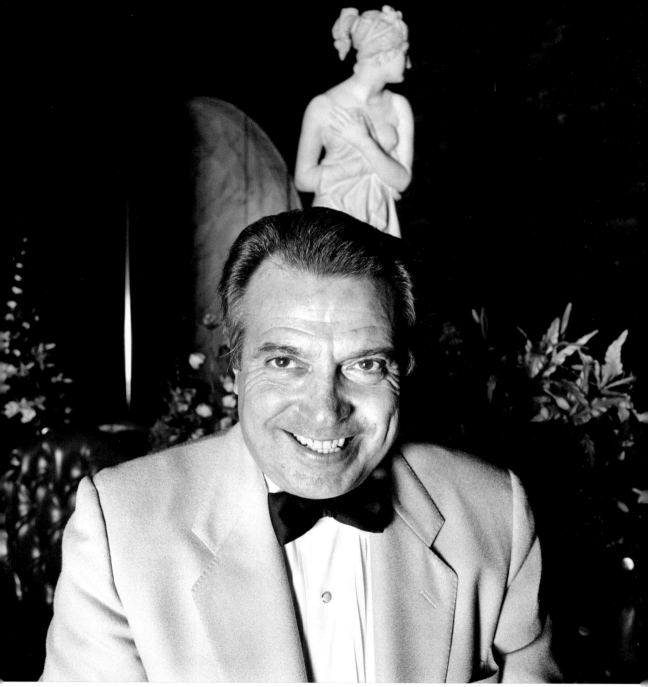

Aldo Bovero, owner of Aldo's Restaurant, Sacramento, California. (1989)

From "Signals"

As their first of the extravagances they had planned for that evening, Wayne and Caroline went to Aldo's, an elegant new restaurant north a good distance. They passed through a tiny walled garden with small pieces of statuary and were met by a tall graying man in a dark suit who said, "Good evening, sir. Madam," and who swung open the heavy door for them.

Inside, Aldo himself showed them the aviary—a peacock, a pair of Golden pheasants, a Chinese ring-necked pheasant, and a number of unannounced birds that flew around or sat perched. Aldo personally conducted them to a table, seated Caroline, and then turned to Wayne and said, "A lovely lady," before moving off—a dark, small, impeccable man with a soft accent.

They were pleased with his attention.

"I read in the paper," Wayne said, "that he has an uncle who has some kind of position in the Vatican. That's how he was able to get copies of some of these paintings." Wayne nodded at a Velasquez reproduction on the nearest wall. "His uncle in the Vatican," Wayne said.

"He used to be *maitre d'* at the Copacabana in Rio," Caroline said. "He knew Frank Sinatra, and Lana Turner was a good friend of his."

"Is that so?" Wayne said. "I didn't know that. I read that he was at the Victoria Hotel in Switzerland and at some big hotel in Paris. I didn't know he was at the Copacabana in Rio."

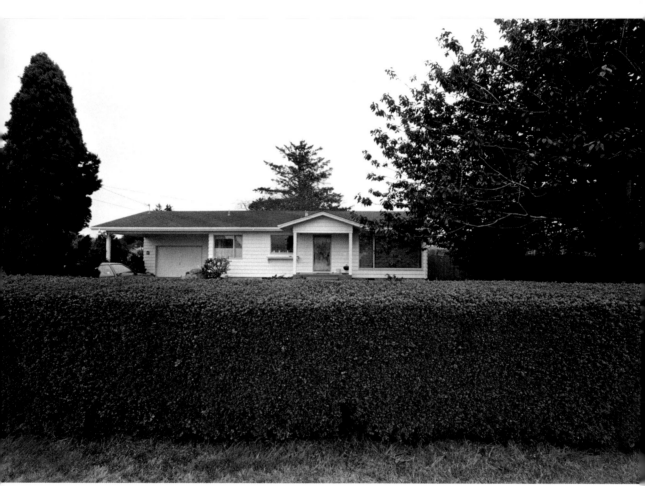

Chef's house, behind the Bella Vista Inn, Arcata, California. (1989)

From "Chef's House"

That summer Wes rented a furnished house north of Eureka from a recovered alcoholic named Chef. Then he called to ask me to forget what I had going and to move up there and live with him. He said he was on the wagon. I knew about that wagon. But he wouldn't take no for an answer. He called again and said, Edna, you can see the ocean from the front window. You can smell salt in the air. I listened to him talk. He didn't slur his words. I said, I'll think about it. And I did. A week later he called again and said, Are you coming? I said I was still thinking. He said, We'll start over. I said, If I come up there, I want you to do something for me. Name it, Wes said. I said, I want you to try and be the Wes I used to know. The old Wes. The Wes I married. Wes began to cry, but I took it as a sign of his good intentions. So I said, All right, I'll come up.

Wes had quit his girl friend or she'd quit him—I didn't know, didn't care. When I made up my mind to go with Wes, I had to say goodbye to my friend. My friend said, You're making a mistake. He said, Don't do this to me. What about us? he said. I said, I have to do it for Wes's sake. He's trying to stay sober. You remember what that's like. I remember, my friend said, but I don't want you to go. I said, I'll go for the summer. Then I'll see. I'll come back, I said. He said, What about me? What about my sake? Don't come back, he said.

We drank coffee, pop, and all kinds of fruit juice that summer. The whole summer, that's what we had to drink. I found myself wishing the summer wouldn't end. I knew better, but after a month of being with Wes in Chef's house, I put my wedding ring back on. I hadn't worn the ring in two years. Not since the night Wes was drunk and threw his ring into a peach orchard.

Wes had a little money, so I didn't have to work. And it turned out Chef was letting us have the house for almost nothing. We didn't have a telephone. We paid the gas and light and shopped for specials at the Safeway. One Sunday afternoon Wes went out to get a sprinkler and came back with something for me. He came back with a nice bunch of daisies and a straw hat. Tuesday evenings we'd go to a movie. Other nights Wes would go to what he called his Don't Drink meetings. Chef would pick him up in his car at the door and drive him home again afterward. Some days Wes and I would go fishing for trout in one of the freshwater lagoons nearby. We'd fish off the bank and take all day to catch a few little ones. They'll do fine, I'd say, and that night I'd fry them for supper. Sometimes I'd take off my hat and fall asleep on a blanket next to my fishing pole. The last thing I'd remember would be clouds passing overhead toward the central valley. At night, Wes would take me in his arms and ask me if I was still his girl.

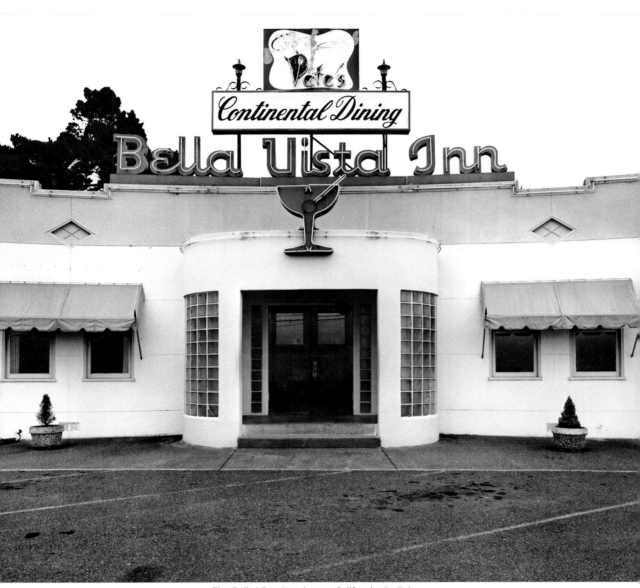

The Bella Vista Inn, Arcata, California. (1989)

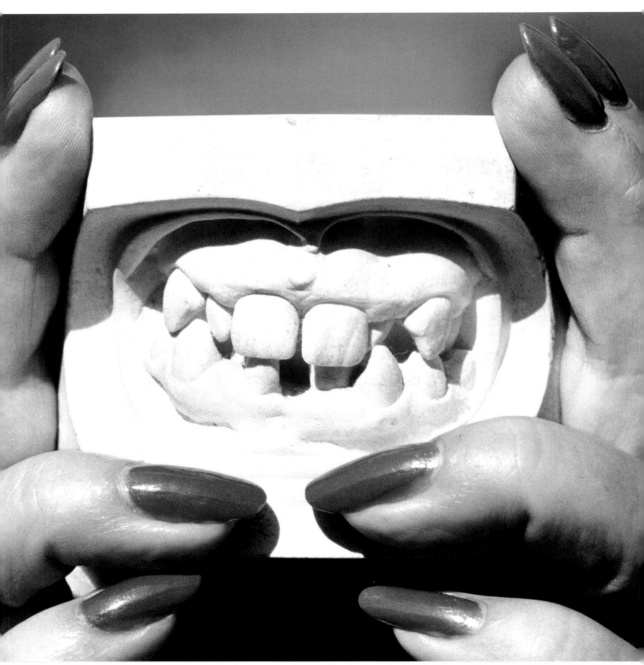

Plaster cast of Tess Gallagher's teeth. (1989)

From "Feathers"

Fran nudged me and nodded in the direction of the TV. "Look up on top," she whispered. "Do you see what I see?" I looked at where she was looking. There was a slender red vase into which somebody had stuck a few garden daisies. Next to the vase, on the doily sat an old plaster-of-Paris cast of the most crooked, jaggedy teeth in the world. There were no lips to the awful-looking thing, and no jaw either, just these old plaster teeth packed into something that resembled thick yellow gums.

Just then Olla came back with a can of mixed nuts and a bottle of root beer. She had her apron off now. She put the can of nuts onto the coffee table next to the swan. She said, "Help yourselves. Bud's getting your drinks." Olla's face came on red again as she said this. She sat down in an old cane rocking chair and set it in motion. She drank from her root beer and looked at the TV. Bud came back carrying a little wooden tray with Fran's glass of whiskey and water and my bottle of ale. He had a bottle of ale on the tray for himself.

"You want a glass?" he asked me.

I shook my head. He tapped me on the knee and turned to Fran.

She took her glass from Bud and said, "Thanks." Her eyes went to the teeth again. Bud saw where she was looking. The cars screamed around the track. I took the ale and gave my attention to the screen. The teeth were none of my business. "Them's what Olla's teeth looked like before she had her braces put on," Bud said to Fran.

"I've got used to them. But I guess they look funny up there. For the life of me, I don't know why she keeps them around." He looked over at Olla. Then he looked at me and winked. He sat down in his La-Z-Boy and crossed one leg over the other. He drank from his ale and gazed at Olla.

Olla turned red once more. She was holding her bottle of root beer. She took a drink of it. Then she said, "They're to remind me how much I owe Bud."

"What was that?" Fran said. She was picking through the can of nuts, helping herself to the cashews. Fran stopped what she was doing and looked at Olla. "Sorry, but I missed that." Fran stared at the woman and waited for whatever thing it was she'd say next.

Olla's face turned red again. "I've got lots of things be thankful for," she said. "That's one of the things I'm thankful for. I keep them around to remind me how much I owe Bud." She drank from her root beer. Then she lowered the bottle and said, "You've got pretty teeth, Fran. I noticed right away. But these teeth of mine, they came in crooked when I was a kid." With her fingernail she tapped a couple of her front teeth. She said, "My folks couldn't afford to fix teeth. These teeth of mine came in just any which way. My first husband didn't care what I looked like. No, he didn't! He didn't care about anything except where his next drink was coming from. He had one friend only in this world, and that was his bottle." She shook her head. "Then Bud come along and got me out of that mess. After we were together, the first thing Bud said was, 'We're going to have them teeth fixed.' That mold was made right after Bud and I met, on the occasion of my second visit to the orthodontist. Right before the braces went on."

Olla's face stayed red. She looked at the picture on the screen. She drank from her root beer and didn't seem to have any more to say.

"That orthodontist must have been a whiz," Fran said. She looked back at the horror-show teeth on top of the TV.

"He was great," Olla said. She turned in her chair and said, "See?" She opened her mouth and showed us her teeth once more, not a bit shy now.

Bud had gone to the TV and picked up the teeth. He walked over to Olla and held them up against Olla's cheek. "Before and after," Bud said.

Olla reached up and took the mold from Bud. "You know something? That orthodontist wanted to keep this." She was holding it in her lap while she talked. "I said nothing doing. I pointed out to him they were my teeth. So he took pictures of the mold instead. He told me he was going to put the pictures in a magazine."

Bud said, "Imagine what kind of magazine that'd be. Not much call for that kind of publication, I don't think," he said, and we all laughed. "After I got the braces off, I kept putting my hand up to my mouth when I laughed. Like this," she said. "Sometimes I still do it. Habit. One day Bud said, 'You can stop doing that anytime, Olla. You don't have to hide teeth as pretty as that. You have nice teeth now.'" Olla looked over at Bud. Bud winked at her. She grinned and lowered her eyes.

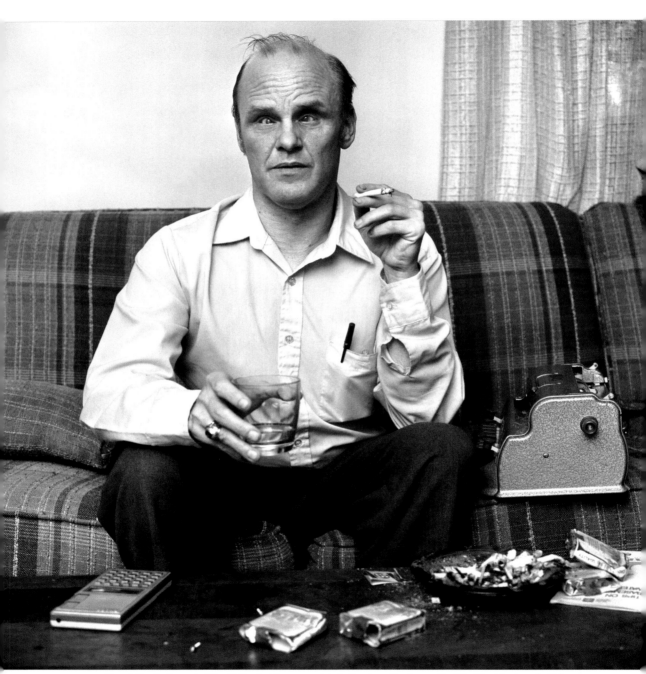

The visitor in Carver's "The Cathedral," was modeled after Jerry Carriveau, Seattle, Washington. (1989)

From "Cathedral"

I've never met, or personally known, anyone who was blind. This blind man was late forties, a heavy-set, balding man with stooped shoulders, as if he carried a great weight there. He wore brown slacks, brown shoes, a light-brown shirt, a tie, a sports coat. Spiffy. He also had this full beard. But he didn't use a cane and he didn't wear dark glasses. I'd always thought dark glasses were a must for the blind. Fact was, I wished he had a pair. At first glance, his eyes looked like anyone else's eyes. But if you looked close, there was something different about them. Too much white in the iris, for one thing, and the pupils seemed to move around in the sockets without his knowing it or being able to stop it. Creepy. As I stared at his face, I saw the left pupil turn in toward his nose while the other made an effort to keep in one place. But it was only an effort, for that eye was on the roam without his knowing it or wanting it to be.

I said, "Let me get you a drink. What's your pleasure? We have a little of everything. It's one of our pastimes."

"Bub, I'm a Scotch man myself," he said fast enough in this big voice.

"Right," I said. Bub! "Sure you are. I knew it."

He let his fingers touch his suitcase, which was sitting alongside the sofa. He was taking his bearings. I didn't blame him for that.

"I'll move that up to your room," my wife said.

"No, that's fine," the blind man said loudly. "It can go up when I go up."

"A little water with the Scotch?" I said.

"Very little," he said.

"I knew it," I said.

He said, "Just a tad. The Irish actor, Barry Fitzgerald? I'm like that fellow. When I drink water, Fitzgerald said, I drink water. When I drink whiskey, I drink whiskey." My wife laughed. The blind man brought his hand up under his beard. He lifted his beard slowly and let it drop.

I did the drinks, three big glasses of Scotch with a splash of water in each. Then we made ourselves comfortable and talked about Robert's travels. First the long flight from the West Coast to Connecticut, we covered that. Then from Connecticut up here by train. We had another drink concerning that leg of the trip.

I remembered having read somewhere that the blind didn't smoke because, as speculation had it, they couldn't see the smoke they exhaled. I thought I knew that much and that much only about blind people. But this blind man smoked his cigarette down to the nubbin and then lit another one. This blind man filled his ashtray and my wife emptied it.

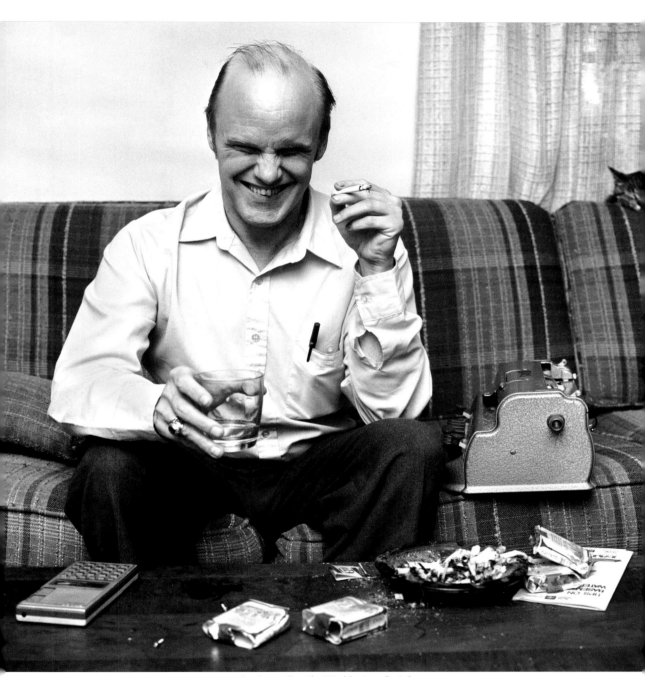

Jerry Carriveau, Seattle, Washington. (1989)

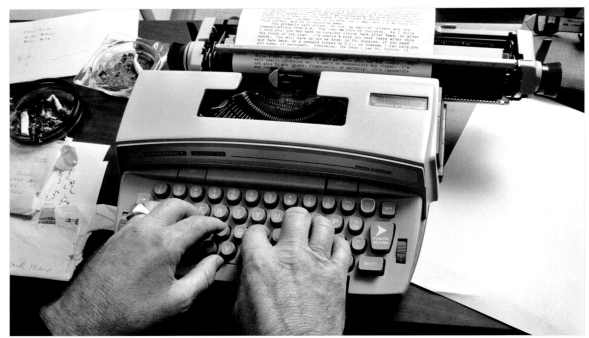

Raymond Carver, Syracuse, New York. (1984)

Work

for John Gardner, d. September 14, 1982

Love of work. The blood singing
in that. The fine high rise
of it into the work. A man says,
I'm working. Or, I worked today.
Or, I'm trying to make it work.
Him working seven days a week.
And being awakened in the morning
by his young wife, his head on the typewriter.
The fullness before work.
The amazed understanding after.
Fastening his helmet.
Climbing onto his motorcycle
and thinking about home.
And work. Yes, work. The going to what lasts.

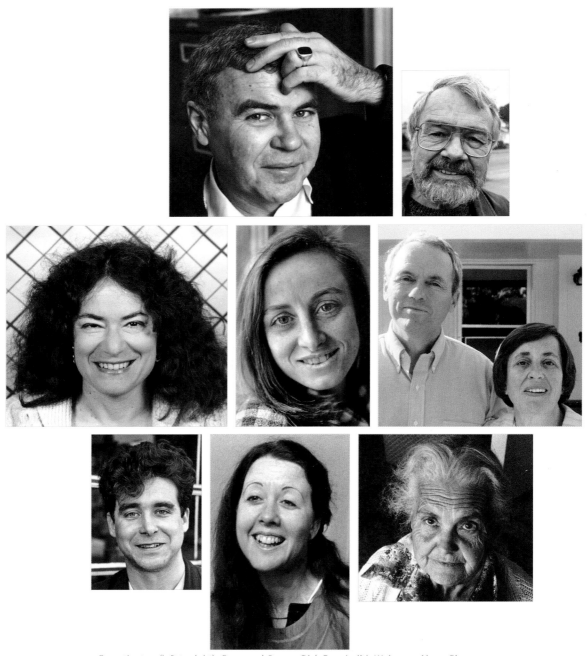

From the top (left to right): Raymond Carver, Dick Day, Judith Weisman, Mona Simpson, Dennis and Loretta Schmitz, Jay McInerney, Tess Gallagher, Georgia Bond

My Boat

My boat is being made to order. Right now it's about to leave
the hands of its builders. I've reserved a special place
for it down at the marina. It's going to have plenty of room
on it for all my friends: Richard, Bill, Chuck, Toby, Jim,
Hayden, Gary, George, Harold, Don, Dick, Scott, Geoffrey, Jack,
Paul, Jay, Morris, and Alfredo. All my friends! They know who
      they are.
Tess, of course. I wouldn't go anyplace without her.
And Kristina, Merry, Catherine, Diane, Sally, Annick, Pat,
      Judith, Susie, Lynne, Annie, Jane, Mona.
Doug and Amy! They're family but they're also my friends
and they like a good time. There's room on my boat
for just about everyone. I'm serious about this!
There'll be a place on board for everyone's stories.
My own, but also the ones belonging to my friends.
Short stories, and the ones that go on and on. The true
and the made-up. The ones already finished, and the ones still
      being written.
Poems too! Lyric poems, and the longer, darker narratives.
For my painter friends, paints and canvases will be on board
      my boat.

We'll have fried chicken, lunch meats, cheeses, rolls,
French bread. Every good thing that my friends and I like.
And a big basket of fruit, in case anyone wants fruit.
In case anyone wants to say he or she ate an apple,
or some grapes, on my boat. Whatever my friends want,
name it, and it'll be there. Soda pop of all kinds.
Beer and wine, sure. No one will be denied anything, on
      my boat.
We'll go out into the sunny harbor and have fun, that's the idea.
Just have a good time all around. Not thinking
about this or that or getting ahead or falling behind.
Fishing poles if anyone wants to fish. The fish are out there!
We may even go a little way down the coast, on my boat.
But nothing dangerous, nothing too serious.
The idea is simply to enjoy ourselves and not get scared.
We'll eat and drink and laugh a lot, on my boat.
I've always wanted to take at least one trip like this,
with my friends, on my boat. If we want to
we'll listen to Schumann on the CBC.
But if that doesn't work out, okay,
we'll switch to KRAB, The Who, and the Rolling Stones.
Whatever makes my friends happy! Maybe everyone
will have their own radio, on my boat. In any case,
we're going to have a big time. People are going to have fun,
and do what they want to do, on my boat.

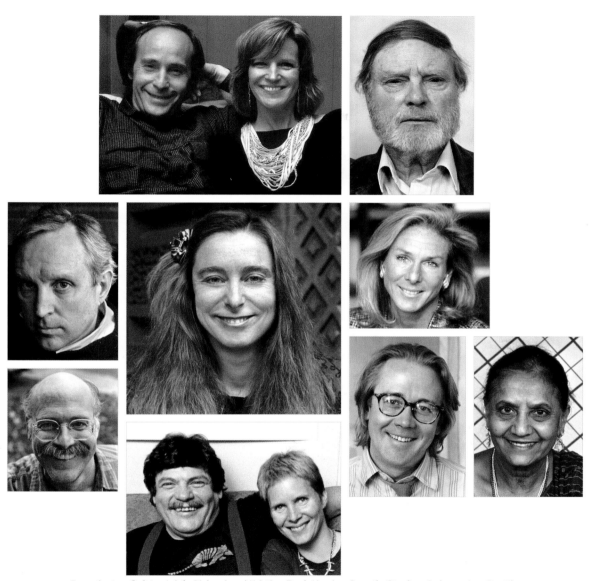

From the top (left to right): Richard and Kristina Ford, Hayden Carruth, Stephen Dobyns, Ann Beattie, Amanda Urban, Tobias Wolff, Alfredo Arreguin and Susan Lytle, Gary Fisketjon, Kashi Wali

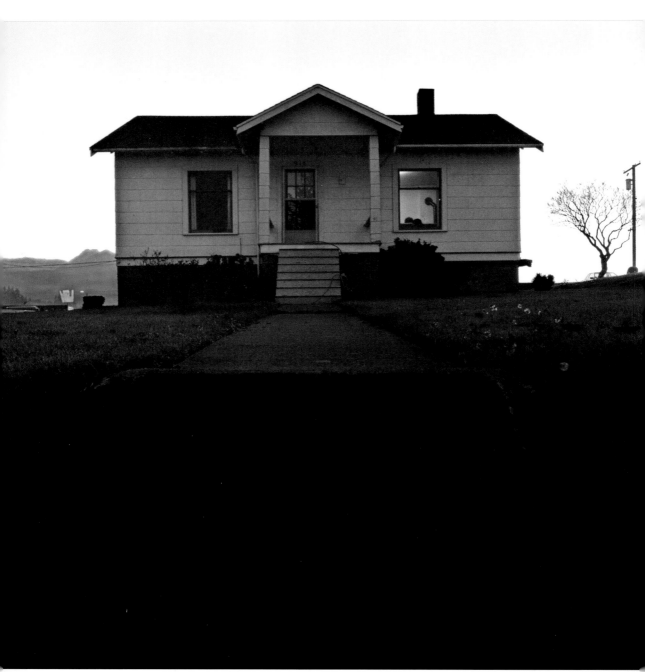

The house in Port Angeles, Washington, where Carver's mother, Ella, lived. (1989)

From "Boxes"

My mother is packed and ready to move. But Sunday afternoon, at the last minute, she calls and says for us to come eat with her. "My icebox is defrosting," she tells me. "I have to fry up this chicken before it rots." She says we should bring our own plates and some knives and forks. She's packed most of her dishes and kitchen things. "Come on and eat with me one last time," she says. "You and Jill."

I hang up the phone and stand at the window for a minute longer, wishing I could figure this thing out. But I can't. So finally I turn to Jill and say, "Let's go to my mother's for a good-bye meal."

Jill is at the table with a Sears catalogue in front of her, trying to find us some curtains. But she's been listening. She makes a face. "Do we have to?" she says. She bends down the corner of a page and closes the catalogue. She sighs. "God, we been over there to eat two or three times in this last month alone. Is she ever actually going to leave?"…

Other people take vacations in the summer, but my mother moves. She started moving years ago, after my dad lost his job. When that happened, when he was laid off, they sold their home, as if this were what they should do, and went to where they thought things would be better. But things weren't any better there, either. They moved again. They kept on moving. They lived in rented houses, apartments, mobile homes, and motel units even. They kept moving, lightening their load with each move they made. A couple of times they landed in a town where I lived. They'd move in with my wife and me for a while and then they'd move on again. They were like migrating animals in this regard, except there was no pattern to their movement. They moved around for years, sometimes even leaving the state for what they thought would be greener pastures. But mostly they stayed in Northern California and did their moving there. Then my dad died, and I thought my mother would stop moving and stay in one place for a while. But she didn't. She kept moving. I suggested once that she go to a psychiatrist. I even said I'd pay for it. But she wouldn't hear of it. She packed and moved out of town instead. I was desperate about things or I wouldn't have said that about the psychiatrist.

She was always in the process of packing or else unpacking. Sometimes she'd move two or three times in the same year. She talked bitterly about the place she was leaving and optimistically about the place she was going to. Her mail got fouled up, her benefit checks went off somewhere else, and she spent hours writing letters, trying to get it all straightened out. Sometimes she'd move out of an apartment house, move to another one a few blocks away, and then, a month later, move back to the place she'd left, only to a different floor or a different side of the building. That's why when she moved here I rented a house for her and saw to it that it was furnished to her liking. "Moving around keeps her alive," Jill said. "It gives her something to do. She must get some kind of weird enjoyment out of it, I guess." But enjoyment or not, Jill thinks my mother must be losing her mind. I think so, too. But how do you tell your mother this? How do you deal with her if this is the case? Crazy doesn't stop her from planning and getting on with her next move.

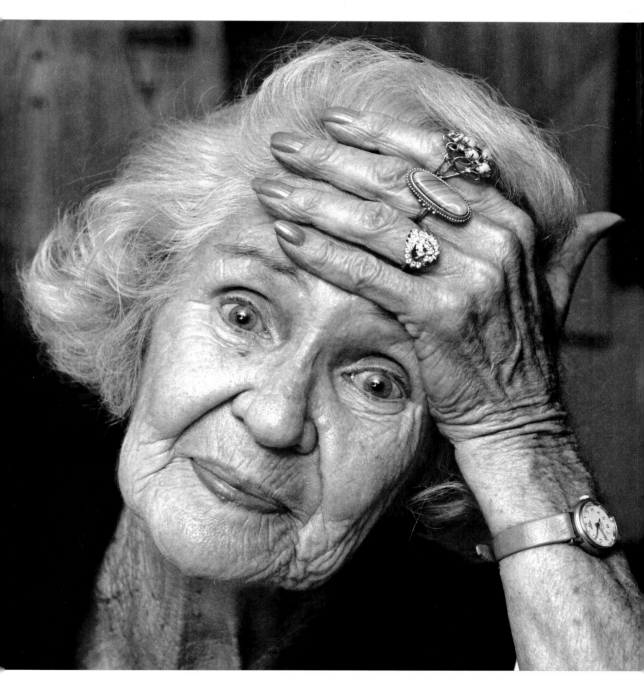

Ella Carver, Ray's mother, Sacramento, California. (1989)

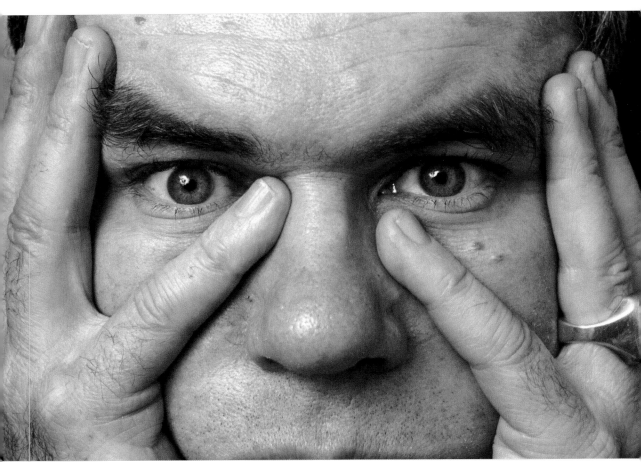

Raymond Carver, Syracuse, New York. (1984)

[From an unpublished letter to Henry Carlile]
September 17, 1986

Just a few lines.... Am feeling a little more than usually embattled here at the moment.... I haven't tried to answer any mail in a week or two—the "guilt pile" as Kinnell calls it—and my mother is spinning out of orbit again; she's planning to move again, if you can believe it. (I'm getting these letters telling me how bad her landlords are—they're not, of course, I spent time with them—how bad and awful the place is, etc. And her plans for the next move, the next apt.) Anyway, I'm being bombarded with these "letters" from her—and asking me why don't I call her, etc. Oh doctors, oh analysts! Where is my shrink? This is insoluble. In AA we used to have a saying, "Let go, let God." This, I think, I'm coming around to seeing, is one of those situations. But then having said that, then what? What now? Let them get my couch ready. Let the doctor prepare to listen carefully, he may never hear such a story again.

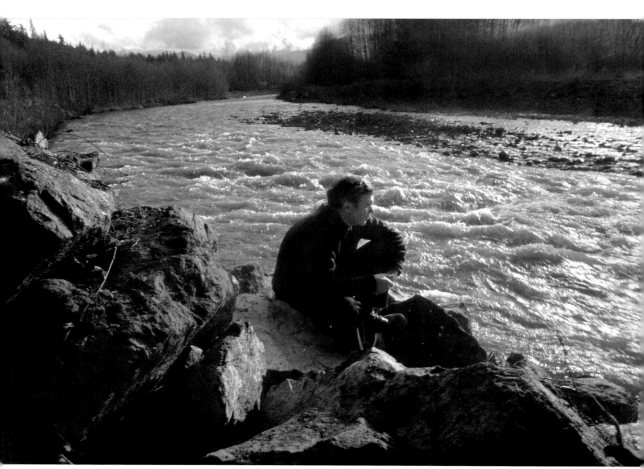

Raymond Carver, Port Angeles, Washington. (1984)

Where Water Comes Together
With Other Water

I love creeks and the music they make.
And rills, in glades and meadows, before
they have a chance to become creeks.
I may even love them best of all
for their secrecy. I almost forgot
to say something about the source!
Can anything be more wonderful than a spring?
But the big streams have my heart too.
And the places streams flow into rivers.
The open mouths of rivers where they join the sea.
The places where water comes together
with other water. Those places stand out
in my mind like holy places.
But these coastal rivers!
I love them the way some men love horses
or glamorous women. I have a thing
for this cold swift water.

Just looking at it makes my blood run
and my skin tingle. I could sit
and watch these rivers for hours.
Not one of them like any other.
I'm 45 years old today.
Would anyone believe it if I said
I was once 35?
My heart empty and sere at 35!
Five more years had to pass
before it began to flow again.
I'll take all the time I please this afternoon
before leaving my place alongside this river.
It pleases me, loving rivers.
Loving them all the way back
to their source.
Loving everything that increases me.

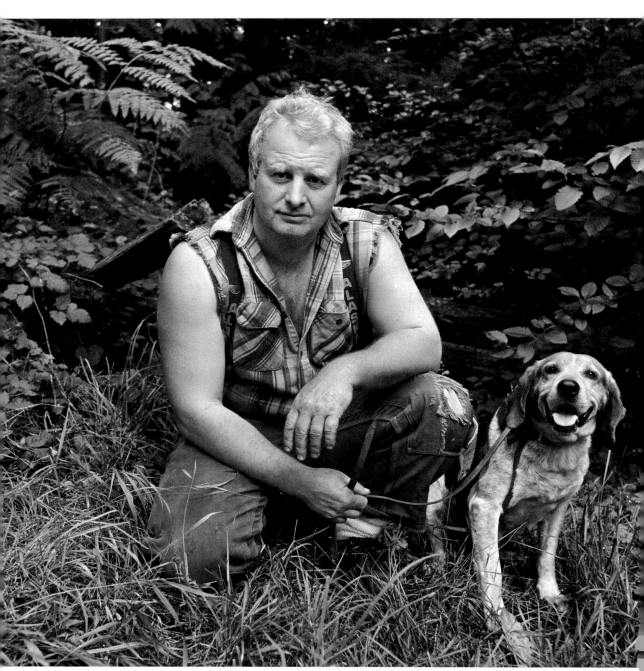

Morris Bond, who set up Elk Camp. (1989)

Elk Camp

Everyone else sleeping when I step
to the door of our tent. Overhead,
stars brighter than stars ever were
in my life. And farther away.
The November moon driving
a few dark clouds over the valley.
The Olympic Range beyond.

I believed I could smell the snow that was coming.
Our horses feeding inside
the little rope corral we'd thrown up.
From the side of the hill the sound
of spring water. Our spring water.
Wind passing in the tops of the fir trees.
I'd never smelled a forest before that
night, either. Remembered reading how
Henry Hudson and his sailors smelled
the forests of the New World
from miles out at sea. And then the next thought—
I could gladly live the rest of my life
and never pick up another book.

I looked at my hands in the moonlight
and understood there wasn't a man,
woman, or child I could lift a finger
for that night. I turned back and lay
down then in my sleeping bag.
But my eyes wouldn't close.
The next day I found cougar scat
and elk droppings. But though I rode
a horse all over that country,
up and down hills, through clouds
and along old logging roads,
I never saw an elk. Which was
fine by me. Still, I was ready.
Lost to everyone, a rifle strapped
to my shoulder. I think maybe
I could have killed one.
Would have shot at one, anyway.
Aimed just where I'd been told—
behind the shoulder at the heart
and lungs. "They might run,

but they won't run far.
Look at it this way," my friend said.
"How far would you run with a piece
of lead in your heart?" That depends,
my friend. That depends. But that day
I could have pulled the trigger
on anything. Or not.
Nothing mattered anymore
except getting back to camp
before dark. Wonderful
to live this way! Where nothing
mattered more than anything else.
I saw myself through and through.
And I understood something, too,
as my life flew back to me there in the woods.

And then we packed out. Where the first
thing I did was take a hot bath.
And then reach for this book.
Grow cold and unrelenting once more.
Heartless. Every nerve alert.
Ready to kill, or not.

To My Daughter

Everything I see will outlive me.
       Anna Akhmatova

It's too late now to put a curse on you—wish you
plain, say, as Yeats did his daughter. And when
we met her in Sligo, selling her paintings, it'd worked —
she was the plainest, oldest woman in Ireland.
But she was safe.
For the longest time, his reasoning
escaped me. Anyway, it's too late for you,
as I said. You're grown up now, and lovely.
You're a beautiful drunk, daughter.
But you're a drunk. I can't say you're breaking
my heart. I don't have a heart when it comes
to this booze thing. Sad, yes, Christ alone knows.
Your old man, the one they call Shiloh, is back
in town, and the drink has started to flow again.
You've been drunk for three days, you tell me,
when you know goddamn well drinking is like poison
to our family. Didn't your mother and I set you
example enough? Two people
who loved each other knocking each other around,
knocking back the love we felt, glass by empty glass,
curses and blows and betrayals?

You must be crazy! Wasn't all that enough for you?
You want to die? Maybe that's it. Maybe
I think I know you, and I don't.
I'm not kidding, kiddo. Who are you kidding?
Daughter, you can't drink.
The last few times I saw you, you were out of it.
A cast on your collarbone, or else
a splint on your finger, dark glasses to hide
your beautiful bruised eyes. A lip
that a man should kiss instead of split.
Oh, Jesus, Jesus, Jesus Christ!
You've got to take hold now.
Do you hear me? Wake up! You've got to knock it off
and get straight. Clean up your act. I'm asking you.
Okay, telling you. Sure, our family was made
to squander, not collect. But turn this around now.
You simply must—that's all!
Daughter, you can't drink.
It will kill you. Like it did your mother, and me.
Like it did.

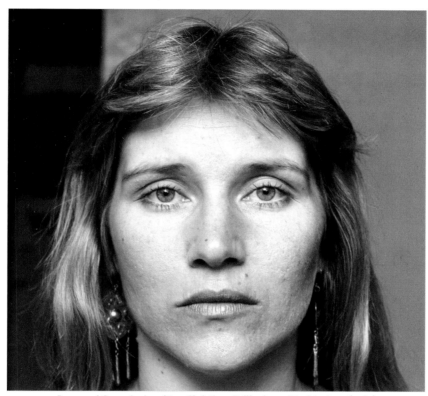

Raymond Carver's daughter, Christine, Bellingham, Washington. (1989)

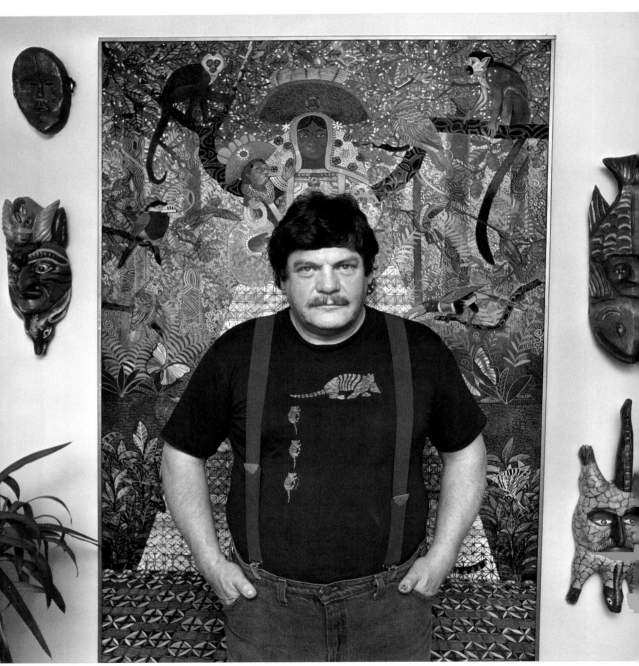

Alfredo Arreguin, a painter who cooks menudo, *Seattle, Washington. (1989)*

From "Menudo"

Once, when Molly was away in that place and I wasn't in my right mind—let's face it, I was crazy too—one night I was at my friend Alfredo's house, a bunch of us drinking and listening to records. I didn't care any longer what happened to me. Everything, I thought, that could happen had happened. I felt unbalanced. I felt lost. Anyway, there I was at Alfredo's. His paintings of tropical birds and animals hung on every wall in his house, and there were paintings standing around in the rooms leaning against things—table-legs, say, or his brick-and-board bookcase, as well as being stacked on his back porch. The kitchen served as his studio, and I was sitting at the kitchen table with a drink in front of me. An easel stood off to one side in front of the window that overlooked the alley, and there were crumpled tubes of paint, a palette, and some brushes lying at one end of the table. Alfredo was making himself a drink at the counter a few feet away. I loved the shabby economy of that little room. The stereo music that came from the living room was turned up, filling the house with so much sound the kitchen windows rattled in their frames. Suddenly I began to shake. First my hands began to shake, and then my arms and shoulders, too. My teeth started to chatter. I couldn't hold the glass.

"What's going on, man?" Alfredo said, when he turned and saw the state I was in. "Hey, what is it? What's going on with you?"

I couldn't tell him. What could I say? I thought I was having some kind of an attack. I managed to raise my shoulders and let them drop.

Then Alfredo came over, took a chair and sat down beside me at the kitchen table. He put his big painter's hand on my shoulder. I went on shaking. He could feel me shaking.

"What's wrong with you, man? I'm real sorry about everything, man. I know it's real hard night now." Then he said he was going to fix *menudo* for me. He said it would be good for what ailed me.

"Help your nerves, man," he said. "Calm you right down." He had all the ingredients for *menudo*, he said, and he'd been wanting to make some anyway.

"You listen to me. Listen to what I say, man. I'm your family now," Alfredo said.

It was two in the morning, we were drunk, there were these other drunk people in the house and the stereo was going full blast. But Alfredo went to his fridge and opened it and took some stuff out. He closed the fridge door and looked in his freezer compartment. He found something in a package. Then he looked around in his cupboards. He took a big pan from the cabinet under the sink, and he was ready.

Tripe. He started with tripe and about a gallon of water. Then he chopped onions and added them to the water, which had started to boil. He put *chorizo* sausage in the pot. After that, he dropped peppercorns into the boiling water and sprinkled in some chili powder. Then came the olive oil. He opened a big can of tomato sauce and poured that in. He added cloves of garlic, some slices of white bread, salt, and lemon juice. He opened another can—it was hominy—and poured that in the pot, too. He put it all in, and then he turned the heat down and put a lid on the pot.

I watched him. I sat there shaking while Alfredo stood at the stove making *menudo*, talking—I didn't have any idea what he was saying—and, from time to time, he'd shake his head, or else start whistling to himself. Now and then people drifted into the kitchen for beer. But all the while Alfredo went on very seriously looking after his *menudo*. He could have been home, in Morelia, making *menudo* for his family on New Year's day.

People hung around in the kitchen for a while, joking, but Alfredo didn't joke back when they kidded him about cooking *menudo* in the middle of the night. Pretty soon they left us alone. Finally, while Alfredo stood at the stove with a spoon in his hand, watching me, I got up slowly from the table, I walked out of the kitchen into the bathroom, and then opened another door off the bathroom to the spare room—where I lay down on the bed and fell asleep. When I woke it was mid-afternoon. The *menudo* was gone. The pot was in the sink, soaking. Those other people must have eaten it! They must have eaten it and grown calm. Everyone was gone, and the house was quiet.

I never saw Alfredo more than once or twice afterward. After that night, our lives took us in separate directions. And those other people who were there—who knows where they went? I'll probably die without ever tasting *menudo*. But who can say?

Is this what it all comes down to then? A middle-aged man involved with his neighbor's wife, linked to an angry ultimatum? What kind of destiny is that?

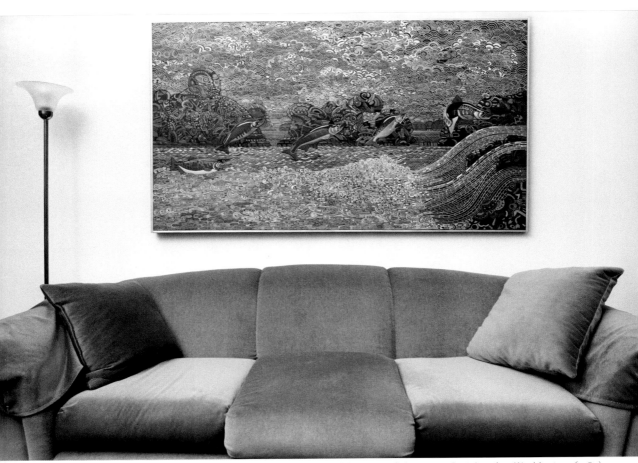

"The Hero's Journey," by Alfredo Arreguin, in Tess and Ray's Ridge House living room, Port Angeles, Washington. (1989)

Dear Alfredo,

I was thrilled to have your letter with your response to "Menudo." I'm so pleased that it pleased you! I haven't shown the story to anyone yet, no one has seen it but Tess, who is my best critic; so your response to the story is important to me, and heartening.... I'm going to send the story off later today to my agent in New York, and I will make the change from "Morelos" to "Morelia." And thank you for catching that and bringing it to my attention.... I'm just awfully happy that you liked the story....

I hope we'll see each other before too long. This is with all love to all of you.

Ray

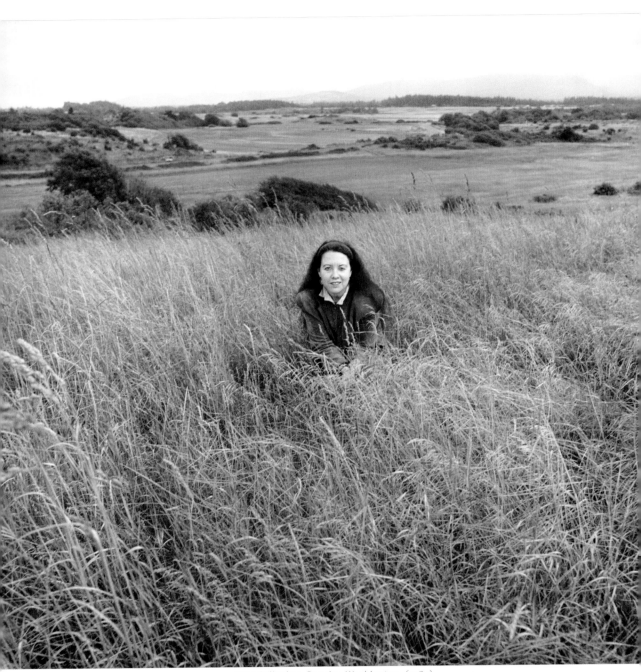

Tess Gallagher, Sequim, Washington. (1989)

In A Marine Light
Near Sequim, Washington

The green fields were beginning. And the tall, white
farmhouses after the tidal flats and those little sand crabs
that were ready to run, or else turn and square off, if
we moved the rock they lived under. The languor
of that subdued afternoon. The beauty of driving
that country road. Talking of Paris, our Paris.
And then you finding that place in the book
and reading to me about Anna Akhmatova's stay there with Modigliani.
Them sitting on a bench in the Luxembourg Gardens
under his enormous old black umbrella
reciting Verlaine to each other. Both of them
"as yet untouched by their futures." When
out in the field we saw
a bare-chested young man with his trousers rolled up,
like an ancient oarsman. He looked at us without curiosity.
Stood there and gazed indifferently.
Then turned his back to us and went on with his work.
As we passed like a beautiful black scythe
through that perfect landscape.

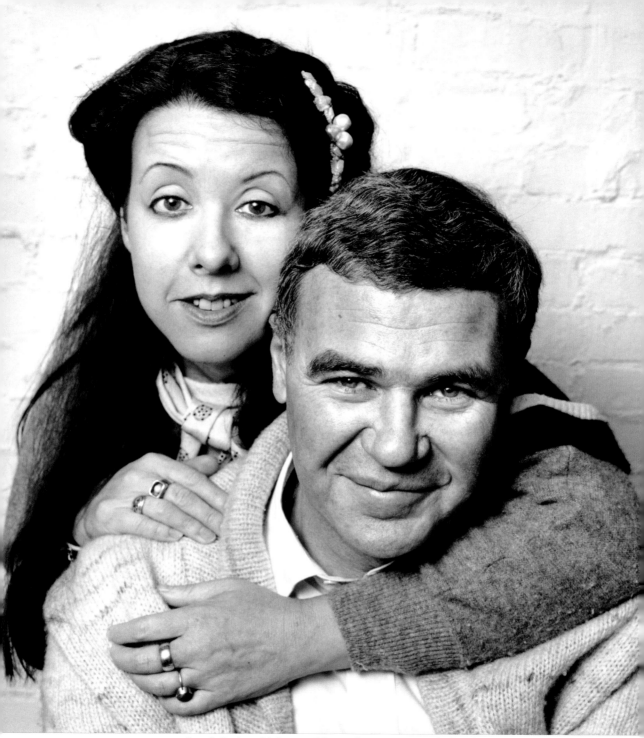

Tess Gallagher with Raymond Carver, Syracuse, New York. (1984)

For Tess

Out on the Strait the water is white capping,
as they say here. It's rough, and I'm glad
I'm not out. Glad I fished all day
on Morse Creek, casting a red Daredevil back
and forth. I didn't catch anything. No bites
even, not one. But it was okay. It was fine!
I carried your dad's pocketknife and was followed
for a while by a dog its owner called Dixie.
At times I felt so happy I had to quit
fishing. Once I lay on the bank with my eyes closed,
listening to the sound the water made, and to the wind
in the tops of the trees. The same wind
that blows out on the Strait, but a different wind, too.
For a while I even let myself imagine I had died—
and that was all right, at least for a couple
of minutes, until it really sank in: *Dead.*
As I was lying there with my eyes closed,
just after I'd imagined what it might be like
if in fact I never got up again, I thought of you.
I opened my eyes then and got right up
and went back to being happy again.
I'm grateful to you, you see. I wanted to tell you.

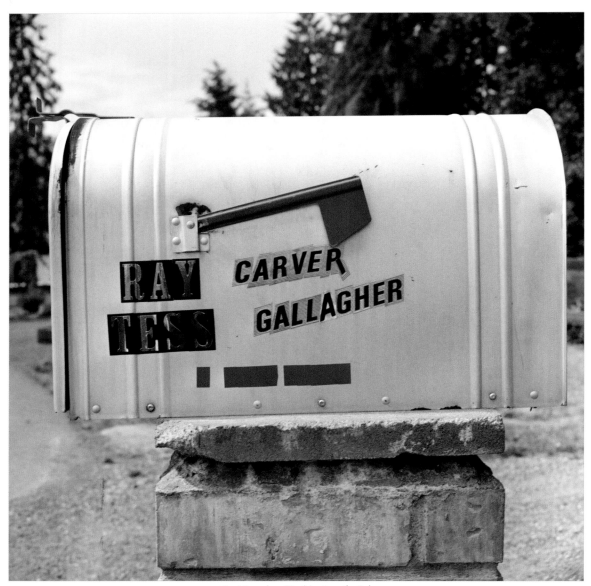

Port Angeles, Washington. (1989)

Hummingbird

For Tess

Suppose I say *summer*,
write the word "hummingbird,"
put it in an envelope, take it down the hill
to the box. When you open
my letter you will recall
those days and how much,
just how much, I love you.

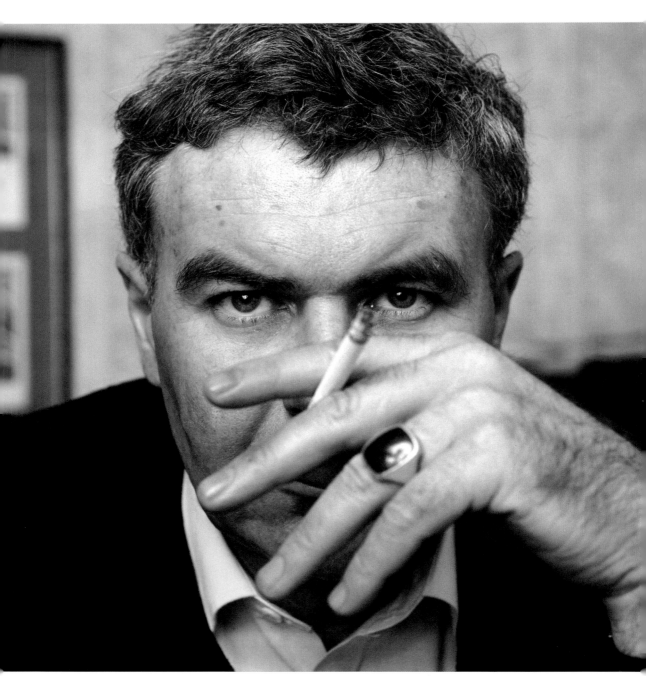

Raymond Carver, Syracuse, New York. (1984)

After-glow

The dusk of evening comes on. Earlier a little rain
had fallen. You open a drawer and find inside
the man's photograph, knowing he has only two years
to live. He doesn't know this, of course,
that's why he can mug for the camera.
How could he know what's taking root in his head
at that moment? If one looks to the right
through boughs and tree trunks, there can be seen
crimson patches of the after-glow. No shadows, no
half-shadows. It is still and damp.…
The man goes on mugging. I put the picture back
in its place along with the others and give
my attention instead to the after-glow along the far ridge,
light golden on the roses in the garden.
Then, I can't help myself, I glance once more
at the picture. The wink, the broad smile,
the jaunty slant of the cigarette.

Gravy

For [that is] what it was ~~Gravy~~ Gravy
~~gravy~~ these past ten years.
Alive, sober, working, loving,
and being loved by a good woman.
Ten years ago ~~the~~ he was told he had
six months to live at the rate he   [but he was going]
was going. So he changed his ways   nowhere
somehow. And the rest? After that ~~the it~~   [cut down]
~~it~~ (was all gravy;   He quit drinking!

Every minute of it, up to and including
when ~~he~~ he was told about ...
"Don't weep for me," he said
I've had ten years longer than ...
Pure gravy and don't ever forget it."

Gravy

No other word will do. For that's what it was. Gravy.
Gravy, these past ten years.
Alive, sober, working, loving and
being loved by a good woman. Eleven years
ago he was told he had six months to live
at the rate he was going. And he was going
nowhere but down. So he changed his ways
somehow. He quit drinking! And the rest?
After that it was *all* gravy, every minute
of it, up to and including when he was told about,
well, some things that were breaking down and
building up inside his head. "Don't weep for me,"
he said to his friends. "I'm a lucky man.
I've had ten years longer than I or anyone
expected. Pure gravy. And don't forget it."

Carver's notebook, Ridge House, Port Angeles, Washington. (1989)

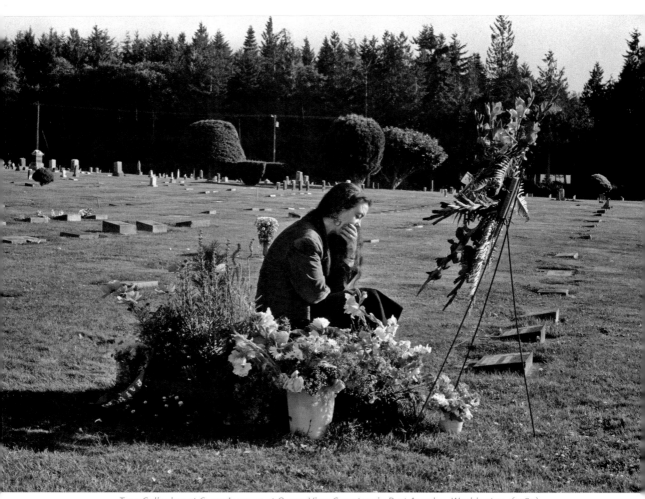

Tess Gallagher at Carver's grave at Ocean View Cemetery in Port Angeles, Washington. (1989)

Late Fragment

And did you get what
you wanted from this life, even so?
I did.
And what did you want?
To call myself beloved, to feel myself
beloved on the earth.

Overleaf: Raymond Carver, Port Angeles, Washington. (1984)

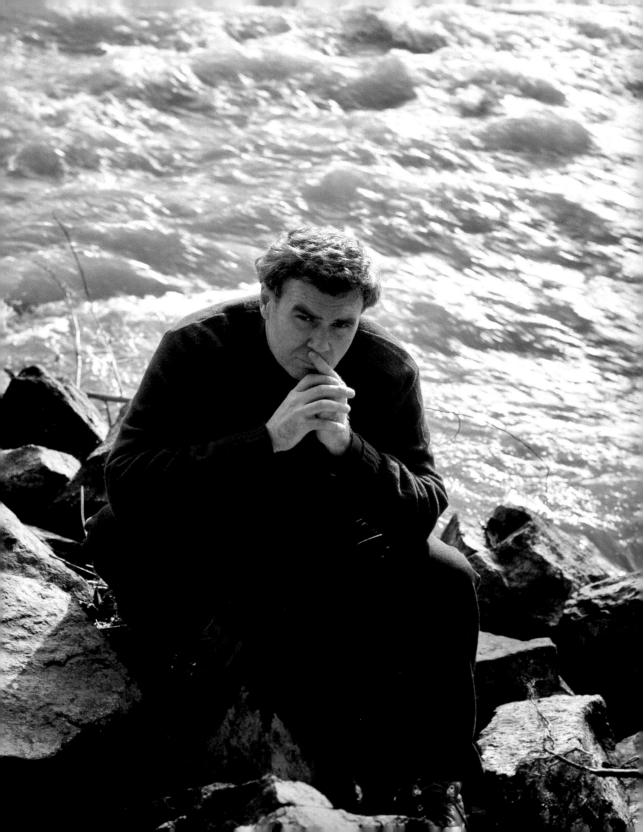

Carver
Country

by
Tess Gallagher

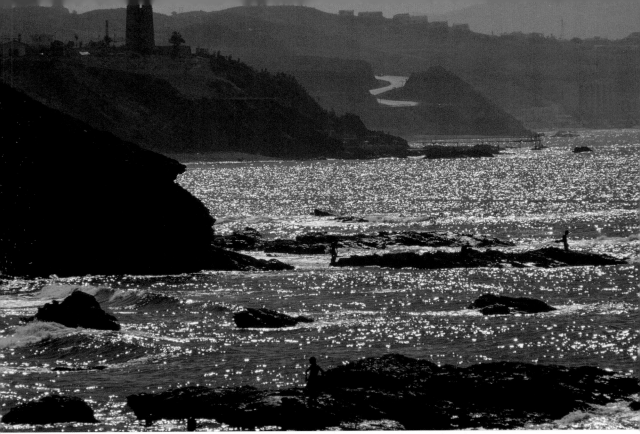

View of the Olympic Peninsula coastline, Washington. (1989)

As Bob Adelman and I set to work on this book I was aware that I felt somewhat baffled as to how to regard the coining of the term "Carver Country"
as it relates to Ray's work and life. It seemed at once integral and antagonis-
tic to our project. That is, I mistrusted the catchiness of its ready-made, haiku-like
smugness, and its seeming assumption that we might be able to locate the qualities
of Raymond Carver's world by simply pointing to physical landscapes out of his
past or to the kinds of people who had appeared in his stories. Nonetheless, the term
became a helpful clue to certain tangible aspects we wanted to define in Ray's work
and, with its limitations in sight, it seemed possible to use it in an exploratory, even
an inspirational, way.

The book gradually began to evolve so that it became more than a collection of
photographs positioned against passages of Ray's work. It became a Story, both of
Ray's life as a writer and a man, and also of our lives together as writers, lovers, and
helpmates. We decided to add selections from Ray's letters, as well as photographs of

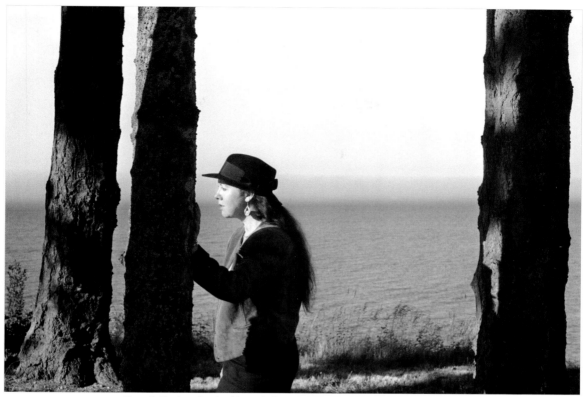

Tess Gallagher, Strait of Juan de Fuca at Port Angeles , Washington. (1989)

his drafts and notebooks, those totemic items he kept on his desk, and photographs of people important to Ray's life.

Finally, as we worked on the book it began to occur to me that Carver Country was, in fact, an amalgam of feelings and psychic realities which had existed in America, of course, even before Ray began to write about them. But because of his writing we began to give these feelings and patterns more credibility. This elusive interior had to be carried in the tonalities of the photographs, in the informal, possibly even furtive, moments of Bob Adelman's artistry. A current of benign menace seemed to pervade Ray's fictionalized world at its inception, and would have to be a strong element in defining the invented territory we are calling Carver Country.

Ray's stories carry their own particular brand of tension—what William Stull, one of the most knowledgeable writers on Ray's work, termed a "purgatorial intensity." Critics have described this ominous quality variously. Marc Chenetier's phrase is a "motherlode of threat." Michael Koepf writes that although there is a Chekhovian

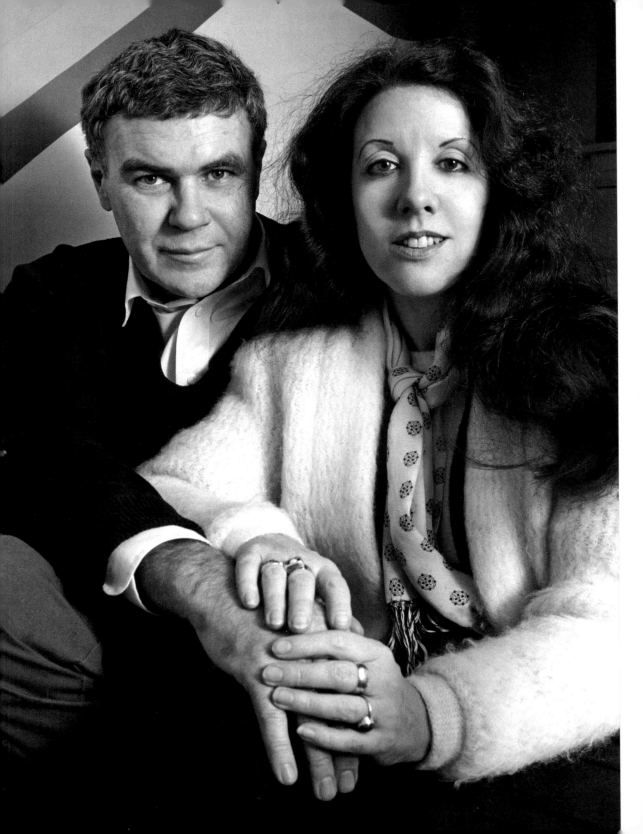

clarity to Ray's stories, there is a "Kafkaesque sense that something is terribly wrong behind the scenes." It is this Kafkaesque quality, combined with the quotidian reality, which I feel Bob Adelman's photographs capture most palpably.

The later expansive, more inclusive and generous aspects of Ray's development have been represented perhaps best in the story aspect of our book—its movement from early life, through his recovery from alcoholism to our marriage and his final days. Bob has approached Ray's writing and life at its most affecting point for his artistic vision, a fact that meant he has focused somewhat more on Ray's early life. This emphasis was also occasioned by a letter Ray wrote to Bob early on in their discussion about the project.

Ray's letter was an encouragement to Bob's work, and its flavor and enthusiasms are so particularly Ray's that it seemed natural that it accompany and explicate many of the photographs which form the nucleus of the book. The text of this letter centers around Ray's childhood and early adult life in Yakima in eastern Washington, and moves on to other locales such as the Grand Coulee Dam on the Columbia River where his father had worked, then onward to the rolling hills known as "Horse Heaven" country near Prosser, Washington, commemorated in his poem called simply "Prosser."

The years in which Ray and I made our life together between Port Angeles in northwestern Washington State and Syracuse, N.Y., have been represented in portraits of some of the people close to us from these places. They include my brother, Morris, Ray's hunting and fishing partner; my friend, Jerry Carriveau, who is blind and on whom "Cathedral" was modeled; our painter friend, Alfredo Arreguin; those named in the poem "My Boat," our colleagues and friends in Syracuse, California, and New York City; and also in the portraits of Ray near Hurricane Ridge or at the mouth of Morse Creek as it feeds into the Strait of Juan de Fuca.

The physical proximity to water, in fact, became a source of inspiration for Ray's later poems and his last book, *A New Path to the Waterfall.* The sense of removal and wildness on the forested Olympic Peninsula with the snow-covered Olympic Mountains, bordered by the moody waters of the Strait between Canada and America, allowed Ray the actual solitude in which to write the stories and poems that would enlarge his work, spiritually and artistically. It is amazing to realize that in the eleven years we were together in Port Angeles and in Syracuse he wrote eleven books, having written his initial two books of fiction and two of poetry during a period of twenty years, ten years of which he'd been suffering from alcoholism.

Landscape did ultimately become crucial to the way Bob was able to suggest a forsaken quality in the lives of Ray's characters. There is nothing, for instance, to give cover in the photograph of Wenas Ridge and, in this, it is like the floodlight intensity of Ray's

Raymond Carver and Tess Gallagher at their Maryland Avenue home in Syracuse, New York. (1984)

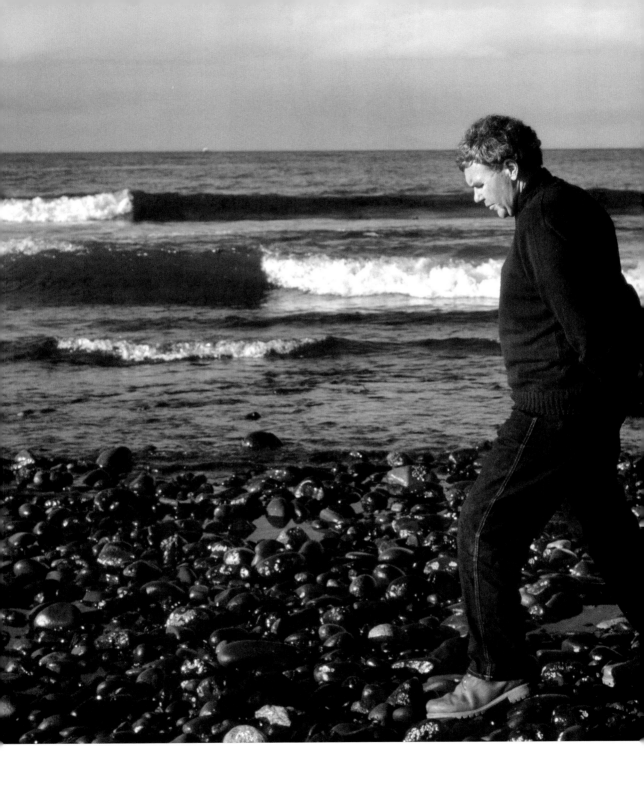

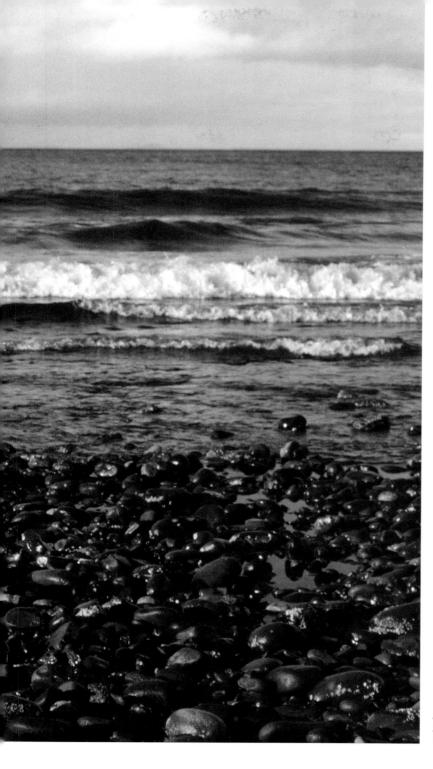

Raymond Carver on the beach below Sky House, Strait of Juan de Fuca, Washington. (1984)

own writing, which put honesty of emotion and truth-telling above all, even to the point of laying his characters' lives open and vulnerable at moments when they were most shamed and overwhelmed. Ray's proclivity for scorning tricks in his writing, for favoring simplicity over ornamentation, for choosing economy as the most telling sign of veracity—these seem present in elements of the Yakima landscape. The complement to this terrain of exposure was perhaps the quiet intimacy Ray found near streams and mountains in Port Angeles, where he lived a good part of his final years.

Ray and I visited Yakima only twice—once in August in 1985 in search of film sites for his story "Tell the Women We're Going," and also to attend his Davis High reunion. On this last occasion we got together with Jerry King, a classmate who'd become a disc jockey, and he and Ray had laughed about what Ray had called their "bozo" days in his poem "The Projectile." Ray's high-school times in Yakima—stealing hubcaps, hanging out with pals Jerry King, Dick Miller, King Cook, and Lyle Rousseau—are mutely present in Bob's photographs of the fairgrounds and of Playland, the shabby music hall where Ray danced to the music of Tommy and Jimmy Dorsey and on his first date got miserably drunk for that first time, and passed out so cold "people thought I had died."

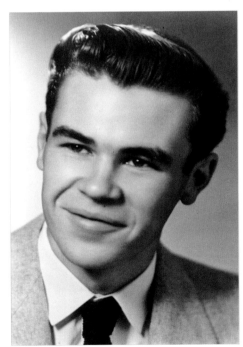

Raymond Carver, high school graduation yearbook

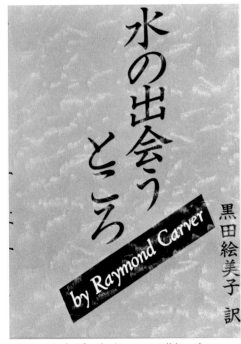

Jacket for the Japanese edition of "Where Water Comes Together with Other Water," translated by Haruki Murakami

Ray had received D's in English and hadn't done much better in his other courses, so it was an amazement to him when his classmates at the reunion recognized him in the program as an "Internationally known writer." When Ray was asked to stand and take their applause he was so happy just to be acknowledged that he fairly beamed.

When I was invited to Davis High after Ray's death, one of the English teachers we'd met at the reunion, Linda Brown, asked me which class I wanted to attend. "Bonehead English," I said, "because that's where Ray would have been." She happened to be teaching such a class, and we read aloud poems by Ray to the students, who put aside their baffled and dazed exteriors for the hour, and entered freshly into the world in which they were living, through the mediation of someone who had sat where they were sitting. I imagined Ray there in the mistakenly near-to-stupid zone, lagging and humiliated, with no bets on him to come out on top in anything.

It was extremely unlikely that a writer growing up in a household where Zane Grey westerns and the newspaper were the only available reading materials would come to affect world literature to the extent that Raymond Carver has. The fact that the stories seem to travel so easily would suggest that Carver Country finds its corresponding territory in the lives of people nearly everywhere. Although his characters were mostly blue collar, especially in the early stories, the appeal of such lives seems not to have limited interest in his stories. Ray was as surprised as anyone to realize that by 1986 his stories had been translated into twenty-three languages, including Japanese, Hebrew, Portuguese, and Dutch. I remember when the first Japanese editions came into the house, how he turned the pages with a kind of bemused astonishment, starting at the back. "Can you beat this," he said. "Isn't this something?"

In France, where the intellectual climate is such that its readers often look askance at writing which doesn't have some pervasive theoretical agenda, Ray's work became highly regarded for its clarity, and a fidelity to reality that quickened its inner strangeness—elements which hadn't been fashionable there since Maupassant, except perhaps in the Nouveau Roman. One of his French translators, Francois Lascan, had originally misapprehended Ray's stance in the stories as ironic. "Then I happened to see a photograph of Raymond Carver and I had to revise my whole idea of his tone and attitude," he told me in Paris. "I knew the man I was looking at in the photograph could never condescend to his characters. I had to retranslate the entire book."

After Ray's death an interviewer for *The Guardian,* James Wood, asked me what I thought had caused Ray's work to come to prominence both in America and around the world during the mid-1980s. In trying to answer I spoke mainly to what was happening in America during the Reagan era and what continues under

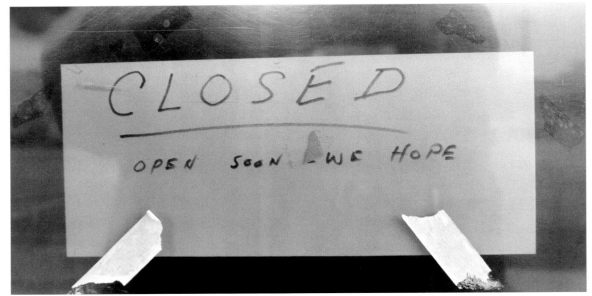

Sign in store window, Port Angeles, Washington. (1989)

both the Bush administrations. Ray's publication had happened to coincide with the fact of the poor having essentially been told to take care of themselves in the guise of the phrase: "the private sector." The private sector was supposed to pick up humanitarian responsibilities the federal government had chosen to drop. It was mostly a verbal dance out of a costly arena for the government. Already the hope, even for middle-class people, of owning a home or of sending their children to college, had begun to slip from their grasp, while this reality for working-class people had hit earlier. If they were out of work and uninsured and fell ill, well it was just their tough luck.

A line from one of Ray's last poems, "His Bathrobe Pockets Stuffed With Notes," represents the embattled situation of many of his characters: "'We've sustained damage, but we're still able to maneuver.' Spock to Captain Kirk." It's this attempt to maneuver, with and in spite of damage, which constitutes the heroic in Carver Country. There is also a phrase which I heard often in my childhood from the working people Ray and I grew up near: "I can't seem to win for losing." This verbal construction inscribes colloquially the two steps forward, three steps backward of life in Carver Country.

It was important to Ray that he give his characters full dignity, no matter how impoverished their circumstances, and I think this is certainly a part of their attraction for readers everywhere. Even when they seem on the verge of being overwhelmed by their struggles or by the ruptures they feel with their surroundings or with their families or mates, they don't capitulate without an assessment of the damage. Ray's

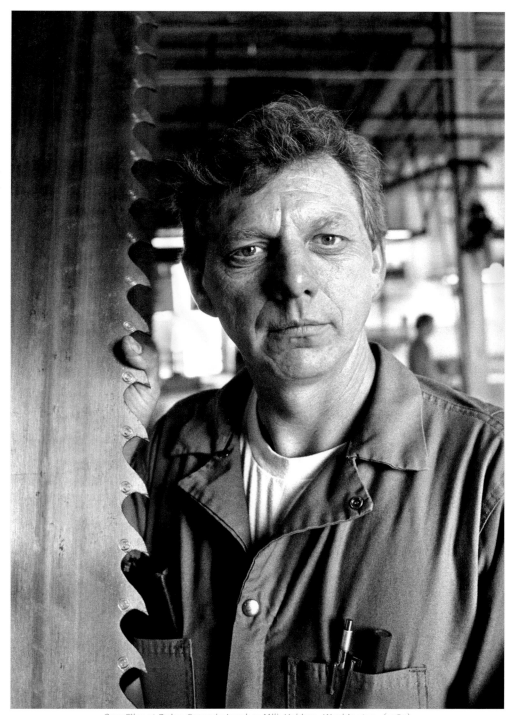

Saw Filer at Boise-Cascade Lumber Mill, Yakima, Washington. (1989)

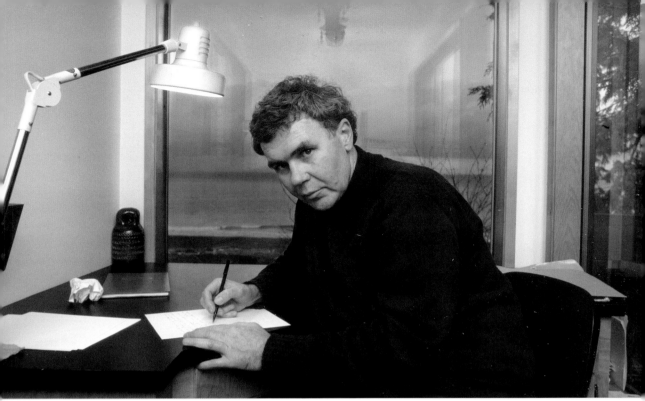

Raymond Carver, Sky House, Port Angeles, Washington. (1984)

stories are a personal record of individual lives lived with no safety net and no imagination of a safety net. The people who are out of work in his stories become more than statistics, for Ray had been one of these people. "I'm a paid-in-full member of the working poor," he'd told interviewers more than once.

W hen Ray and I first met and began to exchange histories he'd told me how, while he was nineteen and raising his young family, both his own parents and the parents of his first wife had taken turns appearing on their doorstep, asking to be taken in. There was the story in his childhood of having had to walk everywhere in the land of the car because his parents couldn't afford to own one. No wonder when, in 1982, we had finished the rewrite of a script on the life of Dostoevsky for Carlo Ponti, Ray took his share of the money and went down to the Mercedes-Benz dealership in Syracuse, N.Y.

He had never had a car that worked. He was wearing a brown V-necked sweater which he'd worn when I'd met him in Dallas in 1977, but the elbows had worn through. It was fall 1982 and just before the summer when he would receive the Mildred and Harold Strauss Living Award, which would allow him five years of writing time free from teaching. He'd told the Mercedes salesman he wanted to try out the latest model. Reluctantly the salesman took him out to the lot and, with the man riding impassively along, Ray was allowed to take the 1983 Turbo Diesel 3000 model for a spin. They drove past the rib take-out places, taverns, and malls, out into the rolling countryside, then turned around and came back. When they pulled up near the showroom Ray noticed, with chagrin, that in his haste to get to the dealer's before closing time he'd come out of the house in his bedroom slippers. No wonder the salesman had looked him over carefully.

"I like it," Ray said to the man. "I like it fine. When can you deliver it?"

"When would you like it?" the man inquired, still rather stonily.

"Would tomorrow be too soon?" Ray said.

"I think we could arrange that," the salesman said, beginning to reappraise the situation. "How would you be paying for it, sir?"

"Is cash okay?" Ray asked.

"Cash is fine," the man said.

He might have pegged Ray as a drug dealer, or maybe he simply felt relieved not to have to substantiate the credit rating of the eager, but rather unlikely looking, customer at his elbow. Ray told me over the phone about buying the car, and he was such a storyteller that every nuance of how he'd made that purchase seems alive in my memory. While all this was taking place I had been nursing my father, who was in the last stages of lung cancer in Port Angeles. That Christmas, Ray drove the Mercedes across the country to Washington and when he arrived we christened it "The Mercedes that Dostoevsky bought."

What made any success sweet for Ray was that in his youth he had lived firsthand the sweat and toil of earning, of working for bosses, the snarl and rip of the green chain at the sawmill, Boise-Cascade, where his father and uncle had worked as saw-filers in Yakima, Washington, during the 1940s and early 1950s. At various periods in his life Ray had assembled bicycles at Sears, picked tulips and hops, run errands for a pharmacy, managed a motel, and swamped floors at a hospital in Arcata. He never forgot the flat-out drudgery, the way these jobs used people up and tossed them aside with little respect for the energies and lives offered there.

Ray knew enough not to think such striving was romantic. Anton Chekhov, his Russian mentor in the short story, had seen it as "the prosaic struggle for existence which takes away the joy of life and drags one into apathy." Ray had experienced from the inside the vagaries of the spirit caused by poverty, too little education, and

Overleaf: Raymond Carver, Olympic Mountains, Washington. (1984)

159

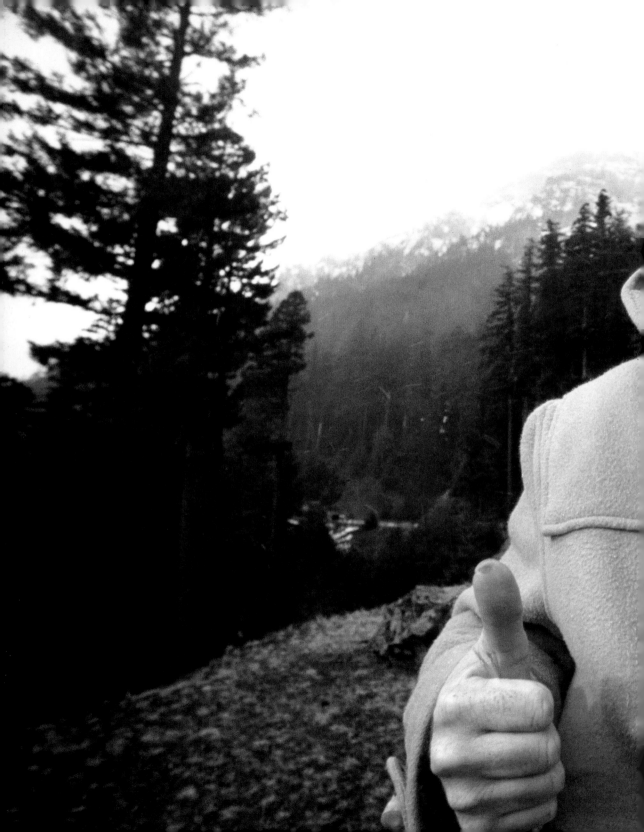

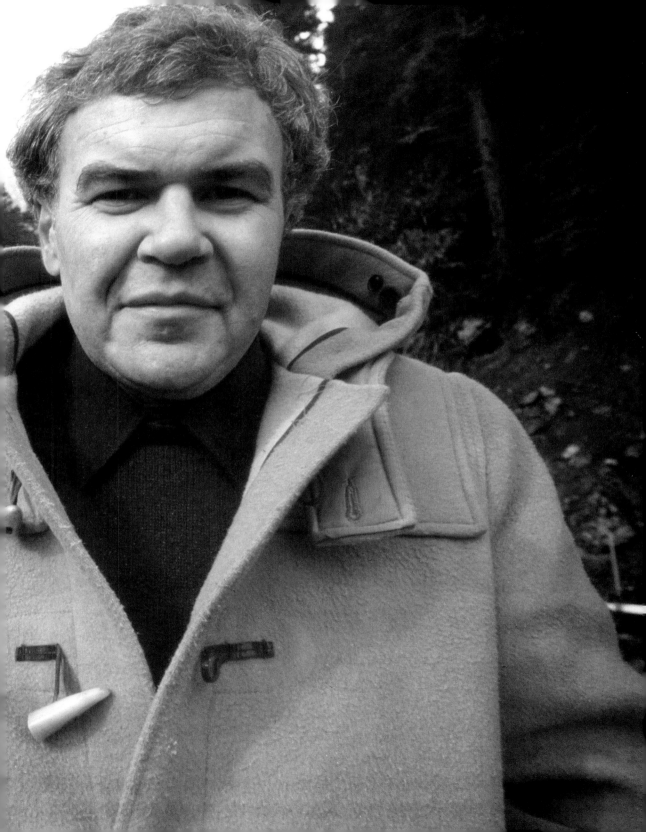

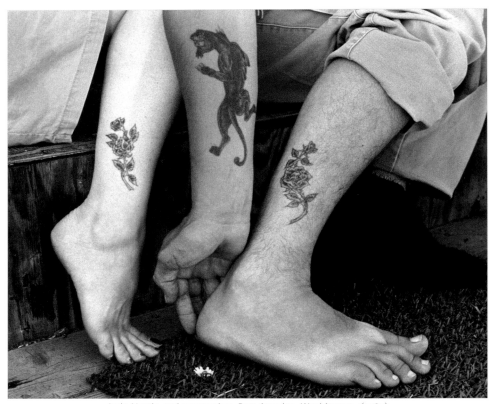

Judy Martin and companion, Port Angeles, Washington. (1989)

a kind of numbness as regards the future which resulted in futile attempts to wall off pain with alcohol. Chekhov wrote, "Peasant blood flows in my veins, and you cannot astound me with the virtues of the peasantry," and Ray was fond of quoting these lines when some naive student or reporter attempted to make him a spokesman for the glories of a working-class existence.

While Ray never forgot these early jobs, he didn't want to go back to that kind of work, and he felt for anyone who didn't have a way out of such a life. What he could do was to communicate that such lives were not without consequence, that the suffering was real and not to be disregarded. He had some inspirational teachers in Dennis Schmitz, Richard Day, and John Gardner, exceptional writers themselves who saw the importance of what Ray was writing, and who stayed by him and encouraged him at a time when few cared whether the people in his stories were ever heard from.

Ray was always alert when anyone was talking about the hardship of work. In his stories he used the jobs people told him about or that he witnessed—my hairdresser, Judy Martin, who stood on her feet from 8 A.M. to 7 P.M. most days and who wore

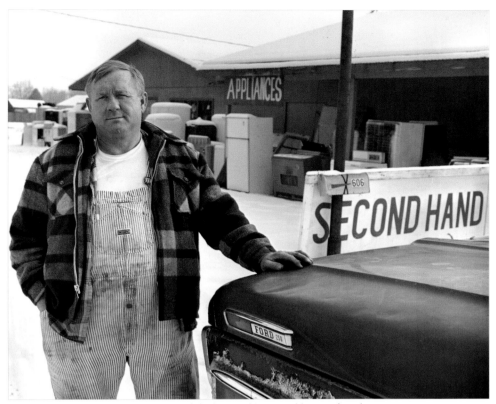

Second-hand dealer in Yakima, Washington. (1987)

a black rose tattooed on her ankle; my brother Morris's work as a gypo-logger and a powder-monkey, setting dynamite off to blast logging roads into the ridge line; the beautiful flight attendant who exclaims in desperation, "I only have two hands" somewhere "over the steaming Mato Grosso"; Ray's janitorial work in a hospital where "a pale and shapely leg" had been left out on a table in the autopsy room he'd been in charge of cleaning; the young fire-eaters we'd seen in Mexico City whose throats had been scorched raw until their voices were lost; the obsessive vacuum cleaner salesman in "Collectors"; harried waitresses and secretaries; women who sold everything from vitamins to the family car; even the strange tweezer-armed photographer in "Viewfinder" who makes his living convincing people to buy Polaroids of their houses.

It was as if the people in Carver Country would have perished without a future tense in the language itself. Carver's people were working or they were out of work. Any day now they "expected to hear from up north" or "people's luck had gone south on them was all." But things were bound to change soon. Things would pick up in the fall maybe." In his stories Ray had been able, in a likeness to the voices and perceptions of the people themselves, to reveal the spiritual tenacity by which these people survived in spite of their limited means, and his readers at all economic levels of the population had been moved toward new awareness.

Surely Carver Country includes those who have disappeared into the powerlessness of alcohol for long tortured periods, some of whom sadly never emerge into sobriety, because the disease, at its worst, seems to require a near-death capitulation before its sufferers will surrender and move toward recovery. In Ray's own case he was hospitalized twice, the last time near kidney and liver failure. He was told on this occasion that he would certainly die, and soon, if he continued to drink. Previous to his collapse, Ray had gone drunk to Alcoholics Anonymous meetings, and after his release from the hospital he'd gone to Duffy's, a treatment center in northern California within sight of Jack London's house. This became the setting for the title story of his last fiction collection, *Where I'm Calling From.*

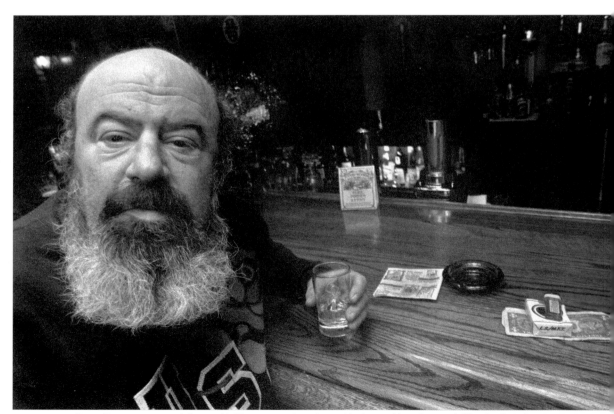

Morry Herman, poet and Carver drinking companion pictured in favored bar, Arcata, California. (1989)

After his stay at Duffy's, Ray "fell off the wagon," partying in San Francisco in the company of friends who missed his drunkenness as an extension of their own. Thankfully he pulled out of it, took himself away from friends and family to a borrowed place he called "Chef's House" in a story he wrote from this period. Alone there, he brought himself down on "hummers," little shot glasses of whisky administered at lengthening intervals.

Gradually he realized it had been a week and he hadn't had a drink; then a month had passed; and by the time I met him for the first time in November of 1977 in Dallas, five months of sobriety had accumulated. He was extremely fragile and, I realize now, that coming to that Dallas writers' conference at Southern Methodist University represented a very big risk for him. Such occasions are always fortified with liquor as the accompaniment to socializing, and Ray braved the overindulgences of others in order to read his stories and to join the company of writers there.

Michael Ryan, a poet and a mutual friend of ours, had invited us to participate in the conference along with Richard Ford, whom Ray was also meeting for the first time, and the poet Philip Levine, among others. I had heard of Raymond Carver and his work from fiction-writing friends in Missoula, Montana, where I'd gone to teach after the breakup of my second marriage. But I had never read his work and we had not met before this time, although we discovered later we had both been in Iowa City where Ray was teaching briefly at the Writers Workshop in 1972, and where I was a student. We had probably ridden up or down with each other in elevators. But as we joked later, it hadn't been time for us to meet.

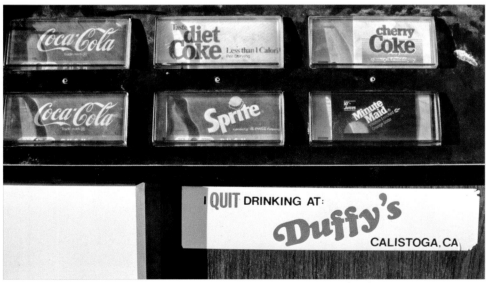

Soft drink machine at Duffy's, Calistoga, California. (1989)

Sitting with poet Jack Myers and other friends in Dallas, listening to Ray read "Fat" and "Why Don't You Dance," I realized immediately that I was in the presence of a sensibility the likes of which I hadn't seen before. His humor, a much over-looked element of his work, combined with a rueful sense of compulsive necessity in "Fat." His gift for the domestically bizarre was also especially poignant for me that day as he read "Why Don't You Dance," in which a man's household goods, arranged room-like for sale on his lawn, become an exposed metaphor of the man's vacated life and marriage.

When I recall Ray standing before us in Dallas, shifting nervously as if he was just able to keep from fleeing the scene, I add to it now what I didn't know then—that this was the first reading he'd given since he'd become sober and, as such, represented a true act of courage. I also add the knowledge, of course, that we would be spending the rest of his life together, and knowing this now, marvel that so little of that future was present for me then, except for admiration of his writing and an affection for the awkwardly gentle man who was so gratefully and humbly before us.

I remember encountering a description of something which had been said of Chekhov to the effect that in his presence people felt they had the ease in which to be themselves, and that even in their weaknesses they would not be judged. All pretense and falsity, all pettiness fell away in his company. This seems an uncannily accurate rendering of the effect Ray had on people as well. His passage through the near-death corridors of alcoholism had left him full of compassion and an ability to love. What was even more winning was that, unlike so many people one encounters, he also knew how to accept love. This somehow communicated itself immediately on sight in his slightly hunched posture and in the shy but attentive way he entered into conversation. He had seen it all and lived to tell it. He never underestimated anyone's pain or struggle. At the same time he never heaped credit upon himself for having overcome his illness. He knew it was a matter of grace, of having put his trust in what AA identifies as "a higher power," and of having miraculously been given the will to turn all temptation to drink aside.

Ray's sobriety was the single most empowering element of his life during our time together. Without that, nothing would have been possible. Ray's state of grace included that the will to drink seemed to have been entirely lifted from him as in the release from a curse. He was not like some recovering alcoholics we knew who were constantly balanced on the precipice of a possible plunge back into darkness.

There was only one time during our life together when I remember being afraid for Ray because of the possibility that he might drink again. This occurred in March of 1988. He'd strangely begun to feel a fearfulness about his sobriety and had started

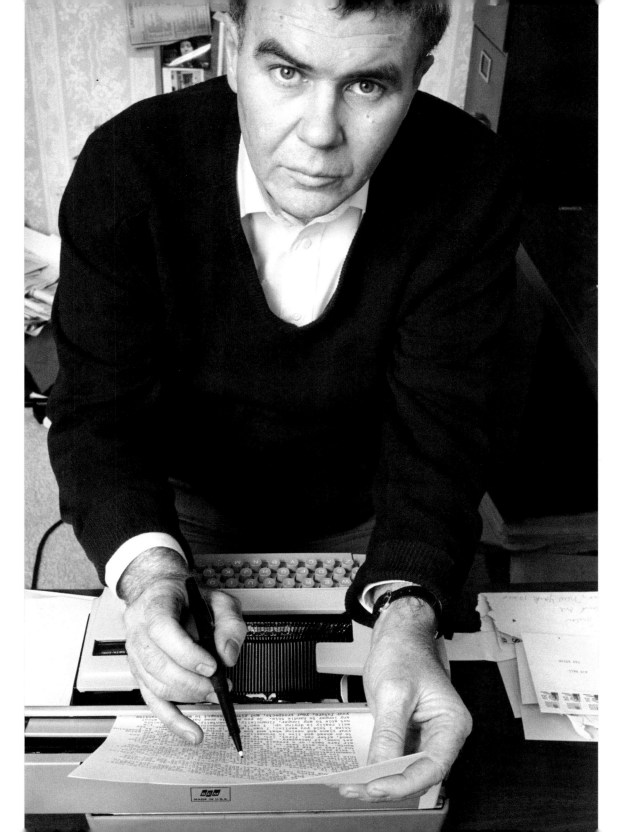

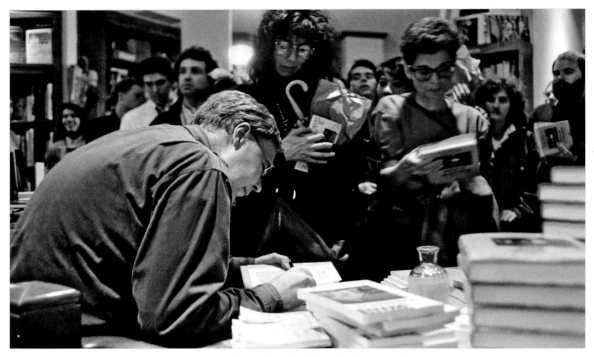

Raymond Carver, New York City, New York. (1988)

out for an AA meeting in Sequim, fifteen minutes from Port Angeles. Not too long after he'd left the house the telephone rang. It was Ray. He had been unable to locate the meeting and had ended up in a bar. "I've ordered a drink," he said, "but I haven't drunk any of it. It's still sitting on the bar." He was like a drowning man reaching out for a life raft. "Don't go back in there," I said, as evenly and as surely as I could. "Come home, hon. Just get in the car and come home." When he arrived home safe and sober, I ran to meet him in the yard and we just stood there a while and held onto each other. "You don't want to go back that way," I said. "Those demons are behind us."

Once the cause of the pressure in his head, the terrible headaches which caused him to lock his jaw, was discovered to be the result of a brain tumor associated with the lung cancer he had been fighting since October, we understood what had caused his brush with the old compulsion to drink. Ray had felt the shame and helplessness of his drinking days, but again he had been allowed an important escape, even during the terrible dilemma of the illness which would ultimately take his life. It meant that he could rightly sustain a vision of himself in his full mental and spiritual strength to the end.

Tess Gallagher, Port Angeles, Washington. (1989)

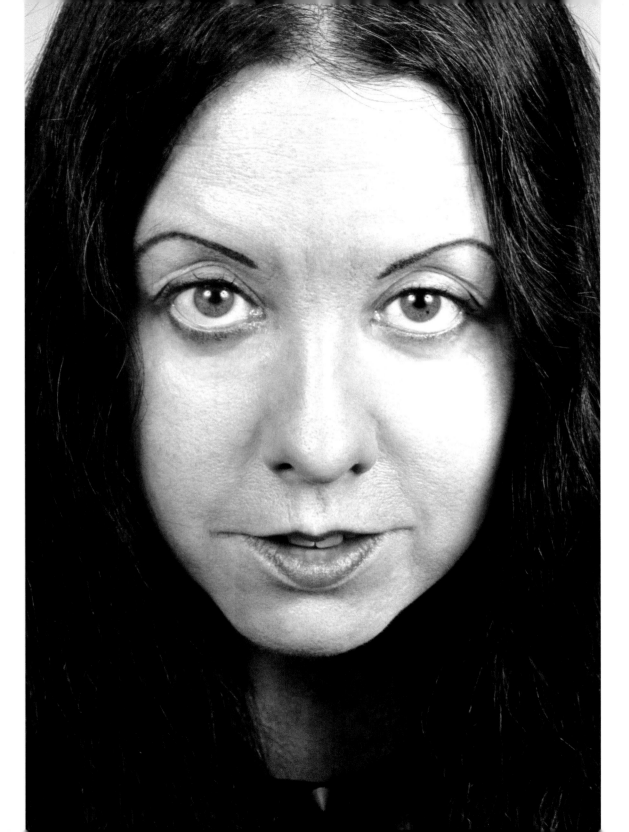

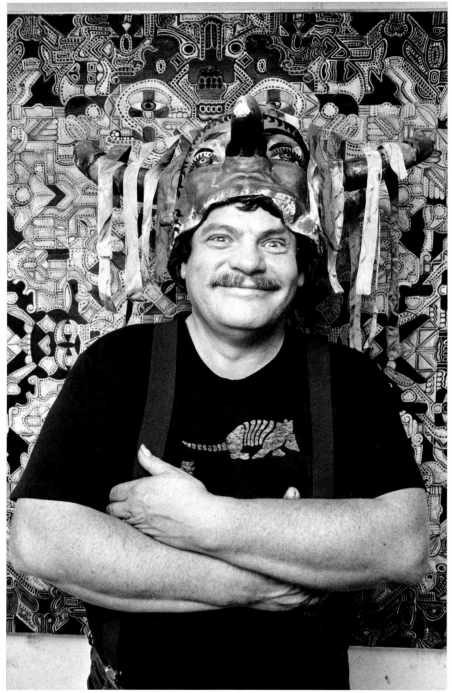

Alfredo Arreguin, Seattle, Washington. (1989)

Ray didn't romanticize what he called his "Bad Raymond" days. But he did maintain an affection for that fallible and wayward self he had preserved most indelibly in his fiction and in stories often recounted in the presence of our friends. I can remember wonderful evenings with the painters Susan Lytle and Alfredo Arreguin in Seattle, during which Ray and Alfredo would be in tears with laughter while sharing some near-catastrophic tale of their separate drinking days.

It had been 1980 when Ray had first met Alfredo, who'd been a friend of mine since I had been seventeen and first in Seattle. Alfredo was still drinking when they met. But, inspired partly by his new friendship with Ray, Alfredo soon gained his sobriety. The two men were like companions who'd been tested in some unheralded but savage campaign, and each time they met there was an aura of the spiritual and physical carnage they had withstood and had miraculously survived. Ray saluted their friendship in the fictionalized character of Alfredo in his story "Menudo." Alfredo's gift to Ray was a painting he had done for us and presented as a wedding gift. It is called "The Hero's Journey" and became the jacket and end-paper art for *A New Path to the Waterfall.* The painting portrays salmon leaping toward a waterfall above patterned magenta waves. In the sky are what Ray called "the ghost fish," a stream of salmon floating in cloud like serenity in the opposite direction. We hung the painting above our couch and meditated often in those last days on its pageantry of struggle and release, which was also, in a sense, a portrait of Ray's own life.

Through his sobriety Ray had been able to improve his own situation, but the fact that he couldn't secure this same release for his family's chronic troubles remained an ongoing heartache. Again and again Ray bent his energies toward consoling and helping his mother and other family members, even when it seemed no good news could come from those quarters.

No matter what stability Ray managed for his own life, it became a fact of life that he would be buffeted and unsettled by the dissatisfactions emanating from the direction of family—which included his mother, his ex-wife, his daughter, and his brother. His son, Vance, had joined us in Syracuse in 1981 to attend college and managed to extricate himself from the marginal prospects of life in the desperate zone.

What one might call the tyranny of family would have to be a main element in any characterization of Carver Country. It figured prominently in Ray's fiction. His characters, whether alone or within marriages or on the periphery of family, have compulsions which arise from the sheer need to be included or remembered. Often they are reduced to simply inventing a usefulness for themselves. These compulsions take hold especially when they find themselves out of work or away from the solace of family. His characters sometimes serve these repetitive, desperate actions as faithfully they might have worked jobs.

There is, for instance, the mother in "Boxes" who moves every few months, and who exemplifies the itinerant or gypsy nature of many of the characters in Ray's stories. Indeed, she represents a facet of American life in the way its people use up "place" and depend upon the idea and the possibility of a "next" or a "new" place as remedy and comfort. In AA shorthand, when an alcoholic does this it's called "taking a geographic," a sign that the drinker is trying to shake his or her troubles instead of dealing with them. But it is entirely possible that moving itself is now inscribed on the national psyche as something "normal" in situations of stress, loss, and despair.

"Boxes" was patterned on the peripatetic movements of Ray's mother, who came, on one of her many moves, to live in Port Angeles near us for a year. During the time I was with Ray he usually spent a couple of months a year in concern over his mother's next move. Her way of installing hopefulness was periodically to shed her surround. These relocations inadvertently guaranteed that she would have the attention and resources of her two sons for a concentrated two-month period each year.

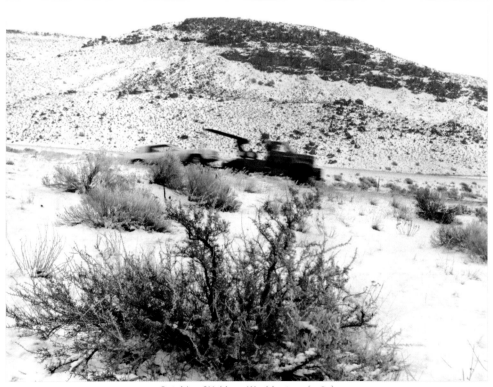

Outside of Yakima, Washington. (1989)

At times the demands from all quarters by Ray's family for money reached such a pitch that he felt his connections with them had been reduced to this—the simple need for cash. The constant din of these requests became the undertow he swam against, voicing his dismay in poems like "The Mail" and "Schooldesk," in which he wrote, "And someone, someone is pleading with me./Saying, 'for Christ's sake, don't turn your back on me.'"

The fact that he had gone on with his life and his writing and had managed to achieve some financial security was, sadly, not a clear good in terms of his family. He balanced the rewards of his success against resentment, accusation, and the easily tapped guilt from the years when his drinking had held him in thrall and had made it impossible for him to give of either means or self.

Ray managed to preserve an attitude of forbearance and love which seemed, even so, to wave like a flag of surrender above what his family required of him. Almost like a litany he would say to me at times, "I don't have a heart anymore where they're concerned. That went a long time ago." Ray and his daughter had in common the specter of alcohol, and having broken free of it himself, he wished nothing less

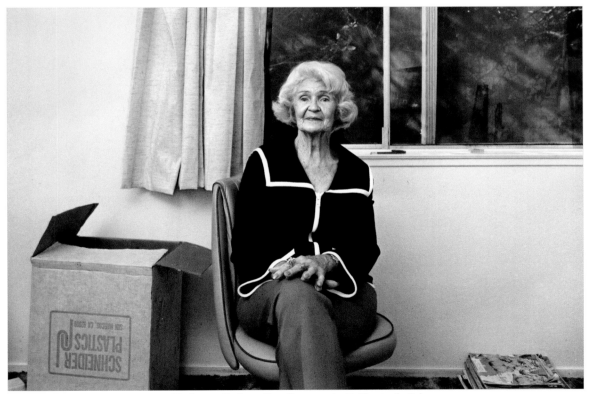

Ella Carver, Ray's mother, Sacramento, California. (1989)

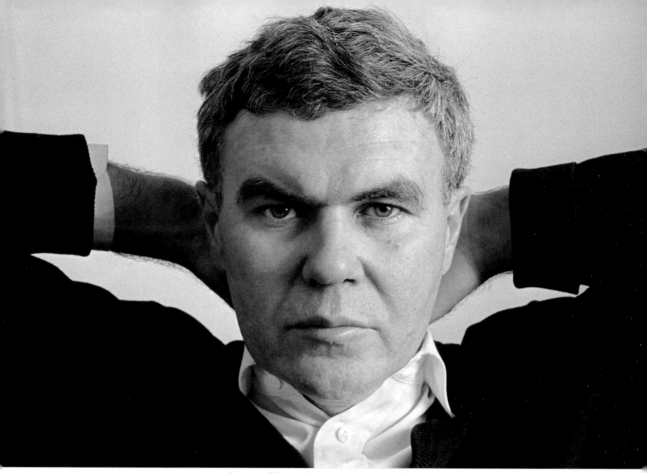

Raymond Carver, Syracuse, New York. (1984)

for his daughter and addressed his concern for her in "To My Daughter," a tough-love poem we've printed with Bob's photograph, and which called out to her not to make the same mistakes he had made.

In one of his last stories, "Elephant," he drew a portrait of a working-class character beset on all sides by the needs of family. The image of the father lifting the boy onto his shoulders and walking with him became central and seemed to ameliorate a conjoining sense of burden, duty, and fractured love presented in the story. As we worked through the drafts, it seemed that Ray and his character reached a kind of equanimity at the center of the unreasonable demands being made upon them. While it is true that the main character's burden is unyielding, he seems to have entered a state of spiritual strength by sheer virtue of his attitude of perseverance and benevolence.

This accommodation and spiritual progress was evident for Ray in relation to his own family, even when they themselves failed to be lifted free. It's never certain what it is that allows for growth in one's character and a tearing away of chaff toward clear vision, but Ray sought more than the petty and meager. He strove in his writing and life not to betray the true hardships of his experience. At the same time he didn't reserve enlightenment for the educated and the self-reliant. His characters might be ignominiously engaged in actions which belonged to the mire, to the partialities of their talents and the laxities of their wills, but he also allowed them their clear moments of recognition and communion when these came, and did so in their vernacular.

One story which was rather a breakthrough for Ray after *What We Talk About When We Talk About Love* was "Cathedral," which he began writing in the fall of 1982 on the train to New York City from Syracuse. My friend Jerry Carriveau had phoned from Maryland to say he wanted to visit us. His wife had recently died of cancer, and he'd come east to spend time with her relatives. Jerry had been blind since birth and in 1970 I'd taken a job working with him for the Seattle Police Department for a year. Our job in the Research and Development Department involved, among other tasks, devising a single-print retrieval file system for fingerprints. In preparation for Jerry's visit, I'd told Ray how I'd drawn fingerprint patterns out on a tablet for my friend in such a way that they formed a raised surface. Then I'd guided his hand over them, simultaneously giving him a verbal description which corresponded to what he was feeling under his fingertips. Ray was masterful in converting this detail when he fictionalized the visit of a blind man in "Cathedral." He caused the blind man's hand to rest on top of the narrator's, thereby placing the narrator in the position of making the recognitions—not the other way around as it had been in the actual instance—and also increasing the intimacy between the characters.

Ray generally hand-drafted his stories in one or two sittings. He secluded himself in his room and appeared only for cups of coffee or to check the mail. But "Cathedral" was drafted on a train paralleling the Hudson River, the very train that Jerry had taken from New York City for our reunion. Ray and I had been given the loan of an apartment for our stay in the city by a friend who was to be away for a few days. This trip was to have been a vacation, a time to see films and plays, and to eat at some good restaurants. It was the first free time we'd had in a long while. But instead of going out on the town, we both fell with a vengeance to our work and didn't venture out except in the evenings.

The apartment was strangely encumbered by an enormous, sleek cat that could stand on its hind legs and knew how to turn doorknobs with its paws. When we attempted to shut it out it would yowl pitilessly and fling itself at the door, or we would hear the click of the latch and feel it pounce onto our bed in the middle of the night. Ray wasn't a cat lover, except for our Persian (which he'd nicknamed "the

Ground Owl"), and the insistent presence of this cat became more and more oppressive. When the cat perched on the sill near an open window one morning Ray began to look longingly out the seventh-floor window to the street below, no doubt imagining its death by accidental means. But in the end we simply wrote and co-existed with the animal, barricading ourselves into the bedroom at night with a chair Ray tilted against the door.

This cat comes back to me as emblematic of how, when I was with Ray, domestic acquiescence could shift subtly toward an unexpected malice, that benign menace so central to his writing.

While we worked together on "Cathedral" a phrase was coined that became a permanent part of our writing vocabulary. It eventually grew somewhat famous as well with our students and colleagues at Syracuse University. One day I had decided to take Ray to dinner at an Irish pub called Coleman's, across town in Syracuse. I'd been there with some students, and the food had been a pleasant surprise after the pub-grub one got in Ireland. We'd started out a bit late and, since I hadn't driven there on my own, I began to hesitate about where I was going. Ray interpreted this as a sign that I was lost and began to despair about ever getting to Coleman's. Anxiety would begin to set in if we didn't get food into

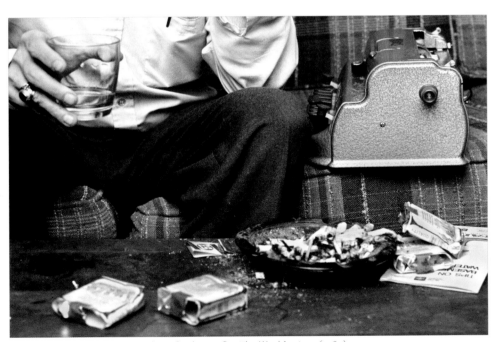

Jerry Carriveau, Seattle, Washington. (1989)

176

him at exactly 5 P.M. each day. Low blood sugar was possibly a problem, though this had never been diagnosed. As we passed a MacDonald's or a Wendy's, Ray would say, "Let's just pull in here, hon. We can go to Coleman's tomorrow." About the time I finally became genuinely lost, he spotted a pizza joint and again attempted to detour us. "Pizza. I'm just in the mood for pizza," he said. "Pizza's just what I had in mind!" Ultimately we reached Coleman's and had a very fine meal, but the journey had left an impression that stayed with us in a new form.

Our habit of working was that once Ray had completed a sufficiently clear, typed version, he would show it to me. When we'd gotten back to Syracuse from our stay in New York he was able to finish a typed draft of "Cathedral" and brought it down to the basement where I was writing one morning. We usually had our conferences in what we jokingly called the "Library," which was just a room where a few of our shared books were kept. We'd sit on the couch side by side and move through each page of the story. But usually, as we began, I'd give a few weather signals about where I thought the story was at this particular stage. That morning I

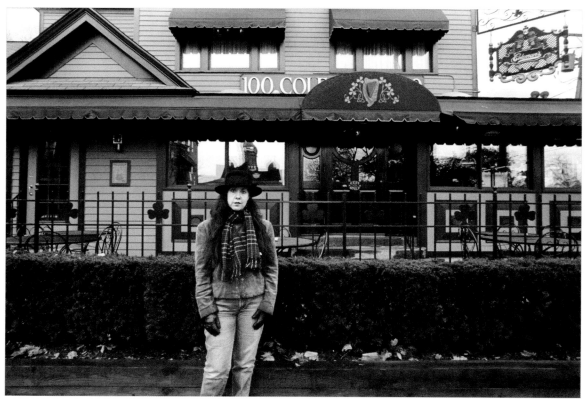

Tess Gallagher in front of Coleman's in Syracuse, New York. (1989)

said, "Ray, this is going to be a completely amazing story, but you haven't gotten it to Coleman's yet. You've stopped at the hamburger stand." We both began to laugh because he knew exactly what I meant. The phrase "getting it to Coleman's" became talismanic between us after that. When Ray eventually finished the present ending of "Cathedral" there was a time when I said to him, "Well now, you have really gotten this story to Coleman's."

It was a constant that those who had formerly been minor characters in the country's literature finally stepped fully into center stage in Ray's work. Their inarticulateness did not exempt them from pain and loss which had the ability to move us. I do still remember a certain cocktail party, however, at which a woman had approached Ray to complain that his characters just weren't intellectually stimulating enough to keep her attention. Then, as if that weren't enough, she'd said, "I also find them just too depressing." We were so used to these stock responses that all we had to do was to look at each other a certain way when it happened in company, marking the spot so we could wash it out later alone. But patience had worn thin, maybe because she'd had her say under cover of alcohol, and this time I wanted to say mildly, "Hey, toots, why don't you just pop a Valium and get with the Wittgenstein."

I recall Chekhov's remark in a letter that "melancholy people always write gaily, while the work of those who are cheerful is always depressing." As a writer then, one couldn't have much control over whether the work would be depressing or uplifting since it was a factor of one's opposite nature. Ray's was a naturally buoyant nature and that meant he had the stamina to reflect the difficult terrain of the lives he portrayed. Ray also felt no writer should have to apologize for the stringency of his or her vision, nor did he ever feel obligated to be anyone's entertainment center. He understood instinctively that he was carrying the news about a people largely forgotten at the heart of the country. Their story was often grim and without recourse to the savvy bulwarks of the educated or of the financially secure.

Ray had been bankrupt himself twice by the time I met him. Our first fight was over whether or not he would take my credit card to a conference in New Jersey where it might come to pass that he would have a sudden need for cash. He was sure he could convince people that there was a misprint on the card and that it should really read "Ted" instead of "Tess." He had the instincts of an outlaw with none of the finesse, though when trying to rent a car with him once at an airport I remember being astonished at how quickly he supplied the name of an expensive hotel we weren't staying at in the city, invented a job he didn't have, and slapped down my overextended VISA which miraculously didn't register as such when they checked it.

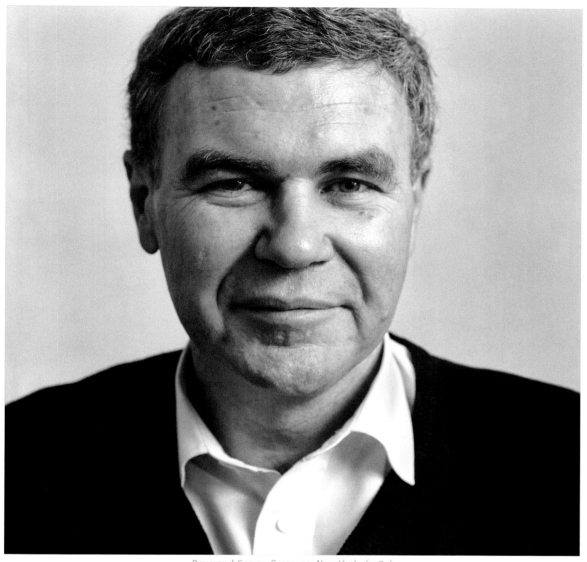

Raymond Carver, Syracuse, New York. (1984)

On another occasion when he'd gotten himself in over his head by committing to go to a conference with me at a time when he flat out didn't want to travel, he'd called his prospective host and told him that his mother had had a stroke. Yes, he was sorry too, but well, it seemed it was out of the question to do anything but to stay by his phone. "Quick," he said to me after hanging up, "what are the symptoms of a stroke? I mean, what happens to you? They're going to call back to see how she's

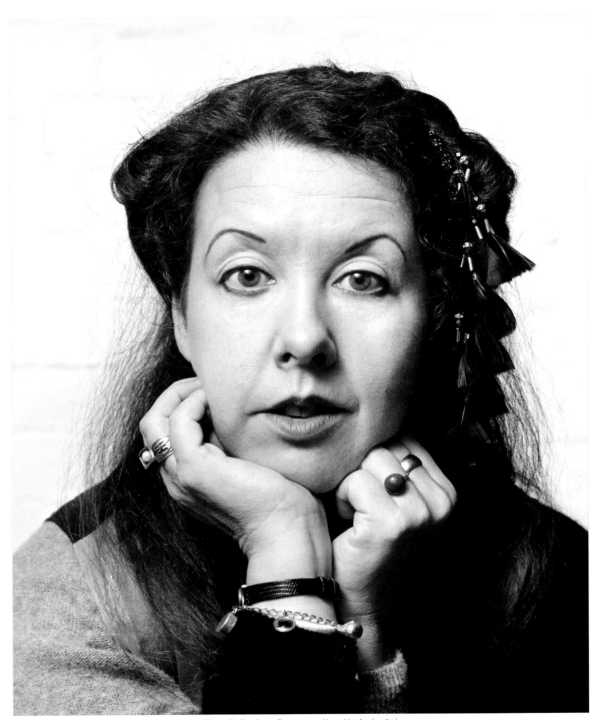

Tess Gallagher, Syracuse, New York. (1984)

doing." I went to the conference alone, having to make daily health reports on Ray's mother who was meanwhile thriving in Sacramento.

The "cover-up," "the side-step," "evasion," and "passing the buck" were all in Ray's bag of tricks when I met him. He'd needed these strategies during his long drinking career. His habit of being on the run from bill collectors had caused him to avoid answering the telephone in our early days. I'd let him off at first, but after a while I made him take his turn at answering it. He'd told me about the police coming to his door in Cupertino, California. They had shouted over a megaphone for all the neighborhood to hear that he should throw out his credit cards and come out with his hands up. "That's behind you," I told him. "We aren't going to live that way now."

I remember feeling afraid when I was first with Ray that living with him might turn out to be like stepping into one of his stories. It seemed that a very thin membrane might separate the world of chaos and order when Ray's perceptions came into play. Some events in our first months seemed to confirm my worst fears, but thankfully this period didn't last long.

My first week in the three-bedroom house he'd rented for us in El Paso in 1979, within sight of the racetrack on the New Mexico border, had begun in a very Carveresque fashion. I was fixing dinner, expecting Ray to come home any minute from his teaching job at the University of Texas, his first job sober. He'd been off booze a year and a half but he was still wobbly on a few essential corners. A knock came at the door and when I opened it a man in coveralls said he was there to turn off the gas. "But I'm cooking dinner," I'd said, appealing to some sense of basic human decency. "I don't make the rules, lady," he said. "The bill hasn't been paid and the gas, she goes off." Carver Country, it seemed, was a zone in which bills, for one reason or another, did not always get paid. Somehow I convinced the man that I would see to paying the bill, and that it wasn't good to make hardships for honest people. But from there on out I took over making sure the bills got paid.

There were times in those first six months together when Ray would get what he called "the willies." This is a state of unaccountable anxiety that is hard to quell and which recovering alcoholics recognize as a danger signal. These feelings will sometimes attach themselves with intensity to otherwise innocent occasions. The night before I was to leave alone on a trip to Ireland in our El Paso days, one of our new friends held a party for us and, much to Ray's consternation, brought out a tarot deck, intending to read everyone's fortune. If someone had produced a live tongue-flicking cobra and proposed we all handle it, I don't think Ray would have been any less terrified. He forbade our hostess to read my cards with a desperation that made you believe in fate, and before she knew what was happening we were into our coats and out the door.

Ray had a strange relationship to luck, to fate, which he loved to test with fishing, by a turn at the racetrack now and again, or at poker with friends. But let one bad sign rear its head in the rest of his life and he was away like a groom blundering into an undertakers' convention. No machine that let him down in those post-drinking days ever got a second chance. If the car sputtered or the dishwasher missed a cycle, out it went.

By the same token, "things" couldn't always rely on him in those days. It was as if objects eluded him in their placid pretence of doing nothing. One day he took a borrowed pick-up to get some furniture that one of our friends had in storage and was loaning to us—it seemed there were many people in El Paso with two or three sets of everything. Ray arrived home with a chest of drawers which had one of the drawers missing. He'd heard of taping them shut but it just hadn't occurred to him. No way did he want to go back onto the freeway to see what had befallen that miss-

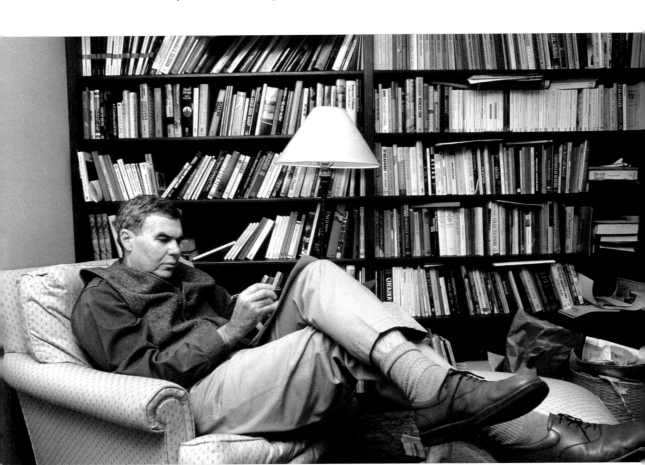

Raymond Carver, Ridge House, Port Angeles, Washington. (1987)

ing drawer. "But that belongs to someone else," I argued. "We have to go back." He didn't see it that way. But he reluctantly drove us to where we found it on a curve, splintered in a place or two but mostly intact.

The following day I glued the drawer together and refinished it. It wasn't perfect, but at least we didn't have a chest of drawers with a gap. That day I sat Ray down for what he would have called "a serious talk." I hadn't planned what I would say, but somehow I knew this was a no-fooling-around matter. "Listen," I said. "I love you. I wouldn't be here if I didn't. But I did not come 4,000 miles across this country to get bad luck. My luck is good," I said, "and I want it to stay that way. You'd better change your luck." I don't know what I thought I was doing—maybe trying to frighten him into a whole new way of life which had no room for the downward spirals he'd been caught in before. I hadn't the least intention of leaving, but I wasn't the daughter of a gambler for nothing, and I could throw a bluff in a way that could make a mouth run dry with certitude that I meant what I said. It was a risk that seems in retrospect to have paid off. Ray did change his luck. Or it changed all on its own.

But the luck of people in Carver Country might be said to be indigenously and hopelessly bad. Their luck has always been bad from the beginning of time and maybe even before time began, and it's easy to feel that no amount of threats or cajoling or solicitousness in their direction is ever going to bring it out of its nose dive. Still, people marooned in Carver Country are under the impression that ultimately they will be rewarded for their patience and suffering. They somehow have been spared the truth that luck settles like a dominion on the worthy and the unworthy, and that the only way it can be kept is by calling on it day and night with the insolence of the bottle for its genii. In the stories Ray wrote, their patience and longings are redeemed as they themselves may never manage in life.

Once Ray changed his luck all things did seem to come to him. During our first year he had thought he might never write again. Early in his sobriety he had even mistrusted his writing, had blamed it for his drinking, and had believed, mistakenly, that it was the cause of his misfortunes—the drinking, the bankruptcies, the end of his twenty-year marriage. Certainly his priorities were right: stay sober and everything else would take care of itself. Gradually he saw that I was writing and decided to try it again himself. By the time we'd moved from El Paso to Tucson in 1980, where I had a job at the University of Arizona, he'd begun to draft the stories which would become *What We Talk About When We Talk About Love*.

He was also feeling strong enough in his sobriety by then that he volunteered to go to AA meetings with one of our friends who confessed he needed help. From time to time over the rest of his life Ray would help others by taking them to meetings, and there's no way to tell how many writers and readers who'd connected

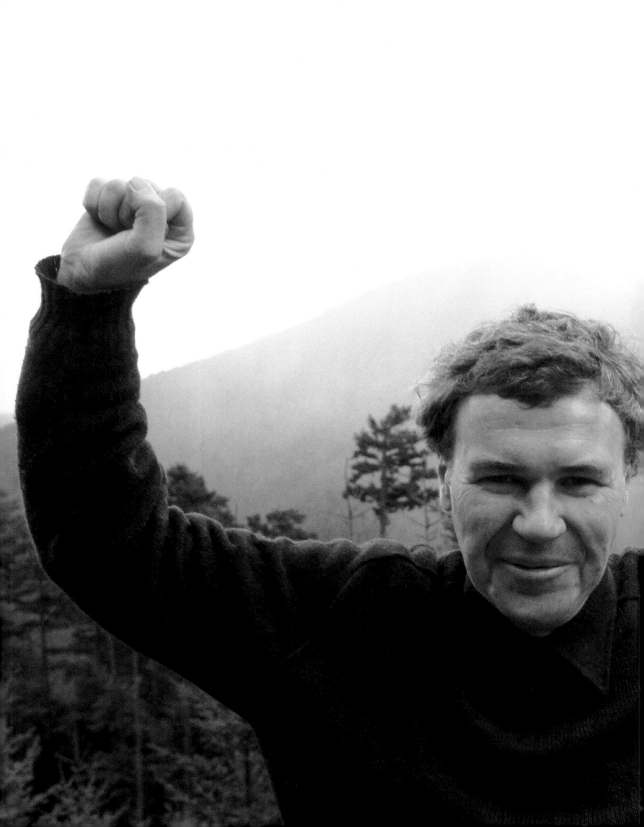

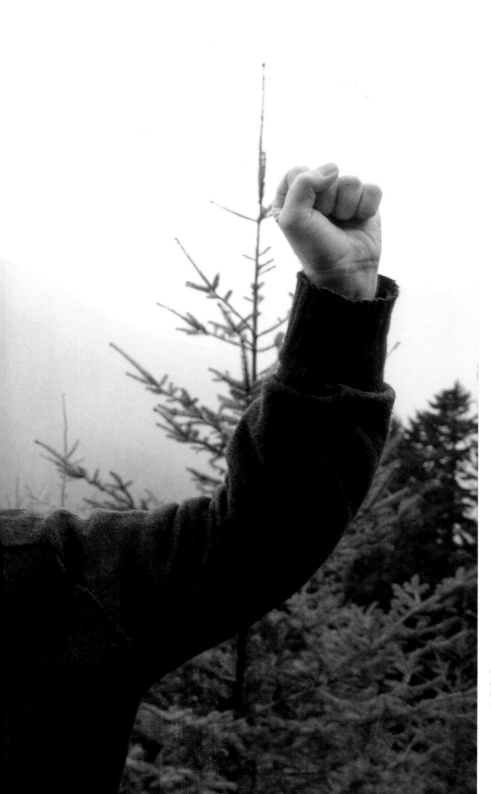

Raymond Carver, near
Round Mountain in the
Olympic Mountains,
Washington. (1984)

with his escape from alcoholism were helped by him through the mails. One such letter found its way to me after his death, and it seemed so indicative of the way Ray reached out to others that we have included it in the text of this book.

In our life together Ray gradually entered a sense of security and stability which had been denied him until then. By 1981 we had a house in Syracuse that we'd bought together, a car that wasn't breaking down every few days, teaching jobs at Syracuse University, and the stories Ray was writing, which would become *Cathedral*, the book which brought him nominations for the Pulitzer Prize and for the National Book Critics Circle Award. With this book Ray's work took on a new richness and dimension, what he saw as a more generous tenor. The spiritual and stylistic growth in this work delivered his writing from the diminishment of the term "minimalist," which Ray had firmly rejected at the start. He preferred the more accurate identification of his style as that of a precisionist. And indeed, critics looking at the entire body of work since have seen the earlier period of *What We Talk About When We Talk About Love* as the most "uncharacteristic" and least representative period of Ray's writing.

As the years of sobriety and literary accomplishment accumulated, Ray's face lost an almost bloated vagueness it had carried when I'd first met him. The jawline firmed up and the muscled places, where humor and a sense of confident well-being had come together, seemed to restore a youthful mischief to his looks. He grew, if possible, even more handsome. His inner pride in himself made him enjoy looking his best. I became his barber early on and clipped away the fluffy sideburns of his drinking days, got him to wear clothes which fit, and for his forty-ninth birthday bought a leather jacket for a trip to Paris, because, I had joked, I wanted him to look like Camus. But in April of 1987 when we walked hand in hand through the streets of Paris on our way to visit Ray's French publisher, our new friend, Olivier Cohen, on the Boulevard St.-Germain, Ray looked like no one but himself—a man in full possession of his life who knew his work was respected. Our love and confidence in each other ran like a current through it all.

The idea to marry had been Ray's. The impetus was the heartbreaking news given by his doctor in Port Angeles that tumors had once again invaded his lungs. Coming as it did, two months after radiation treatments for the brain tumor, it demanded all of our spiritual resources. We had to face the fact that our life together was ending, and yet find courage to live out of and beyond that certain loss. Ray was as brilliant about imaginatively dealing with what was happening to us as the doctor had been at Chekhov's death, in thinking to send down for a bottle of champagne

Raymond Carver, Port Angeles, Washington. (1984)

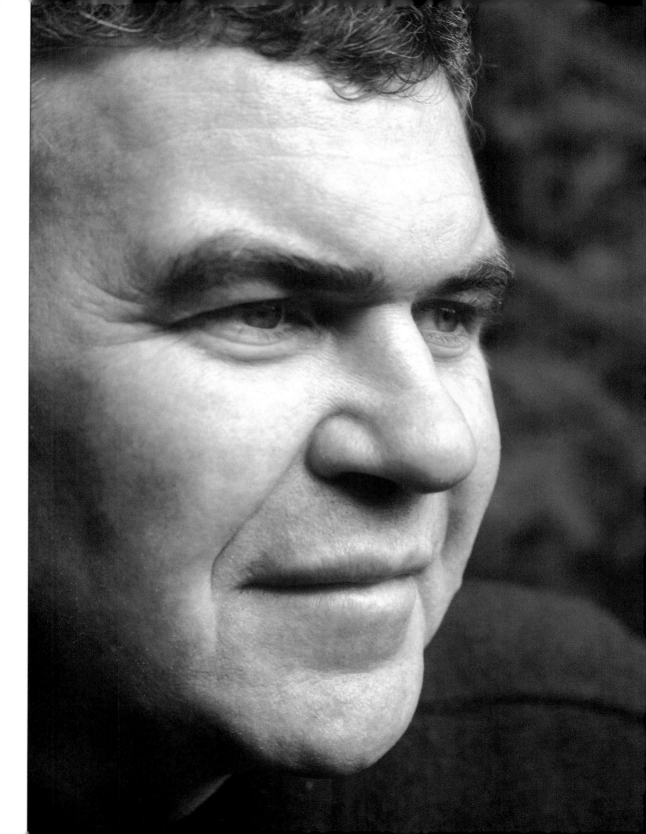

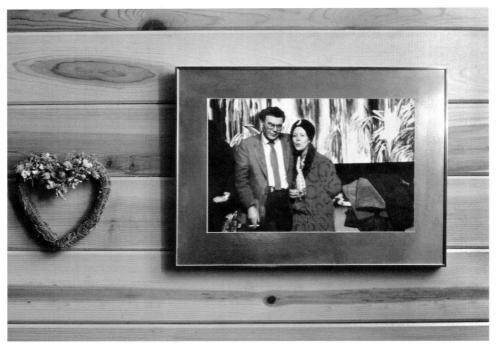

Photograph of Ray and Tess at Harvard University, on display in the room where Carver died, Ridge House, Port Angeles, Washington. (1989)

when a less inspired sort would have persisted in sending for oxygen. "I'll be a corpse by the time it arrives," Chekhov had told his doctor, and the physician had then thought of the right gesture, bringing the celebration of the life forward at its moment of closure. This scene was given in Ray's last story, "Errand," but with a Carver shift of emphasis from the doctor to the waiter who brings the champagne.

So, after eleven years in which our loving had brought about a fusion of energies and spirit while allowing for our own identities apart from each other, we decided to celebrate our relationship by marrying. We bought rings and picked up our plane tickets, told a few close friends, our agent, and my family. Ray wrote to our friend, the poet Henry Carlile, after the wedding in Reno on June 17, 1988, describing this alcove of stopped-time beautifully.

After the wedding at the Heart of Reno Chapel, across from the courthouse, we went to Harrah's to celebrate and I began a three-day winning streak at roulette. We threw ourselves into those days and since there were no clocks to remind us, lost all track of time. I remember on the final morning, just before leaving Bally's (the hotel where we'd stayed), trying to convince Ray to come with me for a last throw at roulette. I had wanted Ray to be with me, as if that final casting of the dice were for him, and because, in some uncanny way, I had known the good fortune of what would happen before it happened. But Ray had already let go of his gambling days and would only half-heartedly play a few slots later at the airport. In some rightness of his own, he wouldn't go into the casino again. He preferred to stand with our luggage, his arms heaped with wedding flowers which had been wired to us by friends abroad, tipped off about the marriage by our agent, Amanda Urban. I hadn't been able to leave the flowers behind.

When Ray saw me running across the casino with my hands full of cash he began to brighten and to shout to me, "Did you do it, hon? Did you win, babe?" The flowers were crushed between us as he hugged me to him in his excitement. "We'll miss our bus," he said in the next breath. "Forget the bus," I said. "We're taking a taxi!"

Our friend Stanley Kunitz, the poet, told me after Ray's death that he couldn't recall any writer or artist during his lifetime who had been so genuinely mourned as Ray was. Besides the plain fact of Ray's genius being gone from the world, part of this outpouring was no doubt due to the fact that Ray was so young—barely fifty. We had all expected and hoped for many more years of his writing and company. It was a life cut short, and we suffered the loss as it was— an aberration, a blow, a chastisement to us all in our faulty assumptions about the future, about mortality and the turns of fate after long struggle.

But loss of Ray seemed to go beyond even the premature fact of it. He was beloved, and luckily he knew this, which somehow extends the benevolence of his presence more surely among us than if he had left in a state of self-banishment, as have some writers. Ray lived his last weeks and days in an urgency of creation, working against the shadows and haltings of his own body as it began to finally give way to the cancer, just managing to complete his final book.

On that last day of his life we played a video tape of the small, intimate wedding reception we'd held with family and friends in Port Angeles after our return from Reno. We laughed at some of the celebration antics during the party, including the escape of our Persian cat, Blue, into raccoon territory. My sister and mother had ended up under the deck on their knees trying to catch the cat and deliver him to safety. Then there was a moment on film where, reaffirming our commitment before friends, we bent to each other and kissed, as we had at our marriage in Reno, long and deeply, while everyone raised their glasses in a toast.

If I could add one element to Bob Adelman's portraits of Ray, it would be something impossible to show in photographs—his infectious laughter. In his years with me the house was full of this laughter, which came out of him as a stored- up gladness, a hilarity that ignited spontaneously while he talked on the phone to friends, or sat in his bathrobe reading aloud from a letter, or just in those domestic moments of companionship where histories have been so absorbed that the humors mix playfully into some heady and rare concoction of twin joyfulness. When I think "never again" of that beautiful sound that was most him for me, I have to be crushed, crushed and uplifted at once. Crushed because it is too beautiful. Uplifted because it is too beautiful to sacrifice to mourning, but must be treasured as that individual breath he was, entrusted to all who shared rooms and hearts with that laughter while he lived. And now again in the reflections and images which join us back to him here.

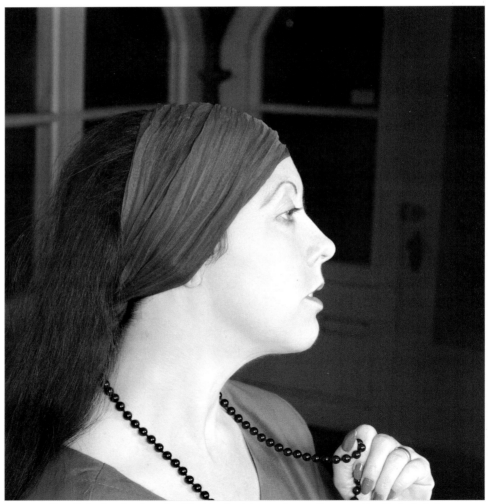

Tess Gallagher, front porch of the Maryland Avenue house, Syracuse, New York. (1989)

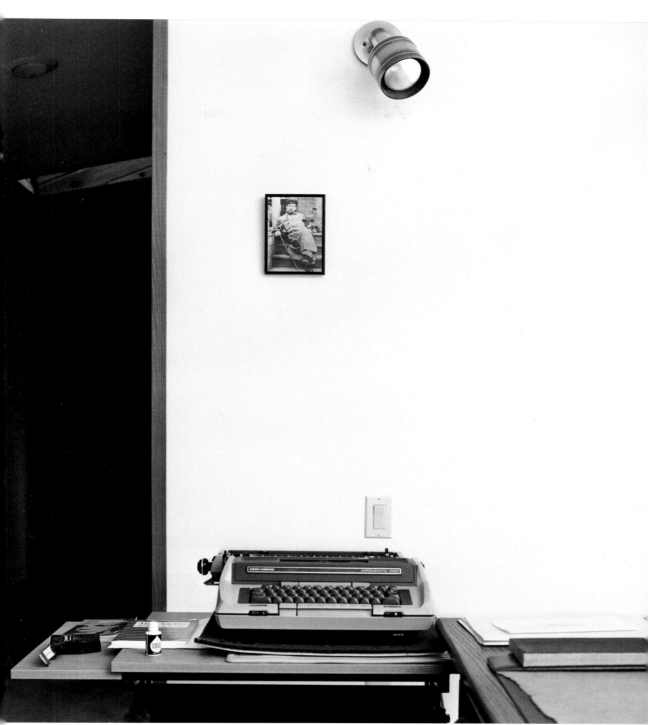

Raymond Carver's desk, Ridge House, Port Angeles, Washington. (1989)

Chronology

1938   Raymond Clevie Carver, Jr., was born in Clatskanie, Oregon, on 25 May, first child of Ella Beatrice Casey and Clevie Raymond Carver, a saw-filer in the Wauna Sawmill.

1941   Carvers move to Yakima, Washington.

1943   RC's only sibling, James Carver, was born in Yakima on 5 August.

1956   RC graduates from Yakima High School in June. He and his mother then follow his father to Chester, California, where RC and his father both work in a sawmill. In November, RC returns alone to Yakima.

1957   On 7 June RC marries sixteen-year-old Maryann Burk in Yakima, where he works as a pharmacy deliveryman. Their daughter Christine LaRae born on 2 December.

1958   In August, RC moves his wife, daughter, and in-laws to Paradise, California, where he enters nearby Chico State College as a part-time student. His son, Vance Lindsay, born on 17 October. RC's first publication, a letter titled "Where Is Intellect?" appears in the Chico State *Wildcat* on 31 October.

1959   In June, the Carvers move to Chico, California. In the fall, RC takes Creative Writing 101, taught by John Gardner.

1960   During the spring semester, RC founds and edits the first issue of the Chico State literary magazine, *Selection*. In June, the Carvers move to Eureka, California, where RC works in the Georgia-Pacific sawmill. In the fall, he transfers to Humboldt State College in nearby Arcata and begins taking classes taught by Professor Richard C. Day.

1961   RC's first published story, "The Furious Seasons," appears in *Selection*, No. 2 (Winter 1960-61). A second story, "The Father," appears in the spring issue of the Humboldt State literary magazine, *Toyon*. In June, the Carvers move to Arcata, California.

1962   RC's first play, *Carnations*, is performed at Humboldt State College on 11 May. His first published poem, "The Brass Ring," appears in the September issue of *Targets*.

1963   In February, RC receives his A.B. degree from Humboldt State. During the spring, he edits *Toyon*. Under his own name he includes the stories "Poseidon and Company" and "The Hair." Under the pseudonym John Vale he includes a Hemingway satire, "The Aficionados," and a poem, "Spring, 480 B.C." RC receives a $500 fellowship for a year's graduate study at the Iowa Writers' Workshop. After spending the summer in Berkeley, where RC works in the University of California library, the Carvers move to Iowa City, Iowa. "The Furious Seasons," revised and republished in the fall issue of *December*, is listed among "Distinctive Short Stories in American and Canadian Magazines, 1963" in *The Best American Short Stories 1964*.

1964–66 In June 1964, the Carvers return to California and settle in Sacramento, where RC is hired as a day custodian at Mercy Hospital. After one year, he transfers to the night shift. In the fall of 1966, RC joins a poetry workshop led by Dennis Schmitz at Sacramento State College.

1967 The Carvers file for bankruptcy in the spring. RC's father dies on 17 June. On 31 July RC is hired as a textbook editor at Science Research Associates (SRA). In August, the Carvers move to Palo Alto, California, where RC meets his future editor Gordon Lish. Martha Foley includes RC's story "Will You Please Be Quiet, Please?" in *The Best American Short Stories 1967*.

1968–69 In the spring of 1968, RC's first book, *Near Klamath* (poems), is published by the English Club of Sacramento State College. Maryann Carver receives a one-year scholarship to Tel Aviv University, and RC takes a year's leave of absence from SRA. The Carvers move to Israel in June but return to California in October. From November 1968 until February 1969 they live with relatives in Hollywood, where RC sells movie theater programs. In February, he is rehired by SRA as "advertising director," and the Carvers move to San Jose, California.

1970 RC receives a National Endowment for the Arts Discovery Award for poetry. In June, the Carvers move to Sunnyvale, California. RC's story "Sixty Acres" is included in *The Best Little Magazine Fiction, 1970*, and his first regularly published book, *Winter Insomnia* (poems), is issued by Kayak Press. On 25 September, RC's job at SRA is terminated. Severance pay and unemployment benefits allow him to write full-time for nearly a year.

1971 In the spring, the San Francisco Foundation selects RC for "honorable mention/special commendation" in its annual Joseph Henry Jackson Award competition. Gordon Lish, now fiction editor at *Esquire*, publishes RC's story "Neighbors" in the magazine's June issue. RC is appointed visiting lecturer in creative writing at the University of California, Santa Cruz, for 1971-72, and in August the Carvers move to Ben Lomond, California. RC's story "Fat" appears in the September issue of *Harper's Bazaar*, and "A Night Out" is included in *The Best Little Magazine Fiction, 1971*. At Santa Cruz, RC serves as founding advisory editor of the magazine *Quarry* (now *Quarry West*).

1972	RC receives a Wallace E. Stegner Fellowship at Stanford University for 1972-73 and a concurrent appointment as visiting lecturer in fiction writing at UC Berkeley. In July, the Carvers buy a house in Cupertino, California.
1973	Appointed visiting lecturer at the Iowa Writers' Workshop for 1973-74, RC moves alone to Iowa City. At the Iowa House, a campus residence, he lives two floors below John Cheever. RC's story "What Is It?" is included in the O. Henry Awards annual, *Prize Stories 1973*, and five of his poems are reprinted in *New Voices in American Poetry*.
1974	RC is appointed visiting lecturer at UC Santa Barbara for 1974-75 and named advisory editor of the UCSB literary magazine *Spectrum*. Alcoholism and domestic problems force him to resign in December, and the Carvers subsequently file for their second bankruptcy. RC's story "Put Yourself in My Shoes" is published as a Capra Press chapbook in August and included in *Prize Stories 1974*. Unemployed, RC returns to Cupertino, California. He remains there with his family for the next two years, during which he does little writing.
1975	"Are You a Doctor?" is included in *Prize Stories 1975*.
1976	*At Night the Salmon Move*, RC's third book of poetry, is published by Capra Press in February. In March, his first major-press book, the short-story collection *Will You Please Be Quiet, Please?* is published by McGraw-Hill under its Gordon Lish imprint. RC's story "So Much Water So Close to Home" is included in the first *Pushcart Prize* anthology. Between October 1976 and January 1977, RC undergoes four hospitalizations for acute alcoholism. The Carvers' house in Cupertino is sold in October, and RC and his wife begin living apart.
1977	*Will You Please Be Quiet, Please?* receives a National Book Award nomination. RC moves alone to McKinleyville, California, and on 2 June he stops drinking. Reunited with his wife, he continues living in McKinleyville through the year. In November, *Furious Seasons and Other Stories* is published by Capra Press. That month, at a writers conference in Dallas, Texas, RC meets the poet Tess Gallagher.
1978	In January, RC teaches a two-week M.F.A. course at Goddard College in Plainfield, Vermont. He receives a John Simon Guggenheim Fellowship, and from March through June, he and his wife live together on a trial basis in Iowa City. They separate in July, with RC leaving for the University of Texas, EI Paso, where he has been appointed visiting distinguished writer-in-residence for 1978-79. In August, he meets Tess Gallagher for the second time, and the two writers begin their close association. RC's book reviews begin

appearing in the *Chicago Tribune, Texas Monthly,* and the *San Francisco Review of Books.*

1979   On 1 January, RC and Tess Gallagher begin living together in EI Paso. They spend the summer in Chimacum, Washington, on the Olympic Peninsula, near Gallagher's hometown of Port Angeles. "From *The Augustine Notebooks,*" a fragment of Carver's never-completed novel, appears in the summer issue of *Iowa Review.* In September, RC and Gallagher move to Tucson, where she teaches at the University of Arizona. RC is appointed Professor of English at Syracuse University in Syracuse, New York. He defers the appointment for one year in order to draw on his Guggenheim Fellowship and write.

1980   RC receives a National Endowment for the Arts Fellowship for fiction. Because of an unexpected retirement at Syracuse, he begins teaching in January, one semester earlier than planned. From May through August, RC and Gallagher live in a borrowed cabin in Port Angeles. In September, the two move to Syracuse, where Gallagher joins the University as Coordinator of the Creative Writing Program. RC and Gallagher jointly purchase a house in Syracuse.

1981   RC and Gallagher continue their routine of teaching in Syracuse from September to May and summering in Port Angeles. RC's essay "A Storyteller's Shoptalk" (later retitled "On Writing") appears in the *New York Times Book Review* on 15 February. His second major-press story collection, *What We Talk About When We Talk About Love,* edited by Gordon Lish, is published by Knopf on 20 April. "The Bath" wins *Columbia* magazine's Carlos Fuentes Fiction Award. RC makes his first appearance in *The New Yorker* with the story "Chef's House," published on 30 November. Thereafter, he becomes a frequent contributor to the magazine. "What We Talk About When We Talk About Love" is included in *The Pushcart Prize, VI.*

1982   During the summer, RC and Gallagher travel to Switzerland. In September, RC's story *The Pheasant* is published in limited edition by Metacom Press. Guest editor John Gardner includes "Cathedral" in *The Best American Short Stories 1982.* (Gardner dies in a motorcycle accident on 14 September.) RC and his wife, separated since July 1978, are legally divorced on 18 October. RC's essay "Fires" appears in the autumn issue of *Antaeus.* Film director Michael Cimino commissions RC and Gallagher to rewrite a screenplay based on the life of Dostoevsky. RC is elected a member of the Corporation of Yaddo, an arts retreat in Saratoga Springs, New York.

1983   Capra Press publishes *Fires: Essays, Poems, Stories* on 14 April. "A Small, Good Thing," RC's original version of "The Bath," is awarded first place in

Prize Stories 1983. It is also included in *The Pushcart Prize, VIII*. On 18 May, the American Academy and Institute of Arts and Letters awards RC and Cynthia Ozick its first Mildred and Harold Strauss Livings: renewable five-year fellowships that carry annual tax-free stipends of $35,000. As a condition of the award, RC resigns his professorship at Syracuse. His essay "John Gardner: Writer and Teacher" appears in the summer issue of *The Georgia Review* and becomes the foreword to Gardner's posthumous *On Becoming a Novelist*. RC's third major book of stories, *Cathedral*, is published by Knopf on 15 September. On 12 December, it receives a National Book Critics Circle Award nomination. RC edits a Special Fiction Issue of *Ploughshares*, and guest editor Anne Tyler includes "Where I'm Calling From" in *The Best American Short Stories 1983*.

1984   In January, RC flees the publicity "hubbub" in Syracuse and moves alone into Gallagher's newly built "Sky House" in Port Angeles. RC writes poetry during the day and occasional nonfiction during the evening. On 22 April, his review of Sherwood Anderson's *Selected Letters* appears in the *New York Times Book Review*. RC contributes a foreword to *We Are Not in This Together: Stories by William Kittredge*. In the summer, he and Gallagher make a reading tour of Brazil and Argentina for the U.S. Information Service. In the fall, they return to Syracuse, where Gallagher arranges to teach only one semester each year. "Purple Lake," an unproduced screenplay written by RC and Michael Cimino, is registered on 10 September. RC's essay "My Father's Life" appears in the September issue of *Esquire*, and his story *If It Please You* is published in September as a Lord John Press limited edition. Seven of RC's poems are reprinted in *The Generation of 2000*, and his story "Careful" is included in *The Pushcart Prize, IX*. *Cathedral* receives a Pulitzer Prize nomination.

1985   In January, RC buys a house in a working-class district of Port Angeles. He and Gallagher share their two residences in Port Angeles from January through August, and in September they return to Syracuse. Five of RC's poems appear in the February issue of *Poetry* (Chicago). Thereafter, he becomes a regular contributor. Random House publishes RC's poetry collection *Where Water Comes Together with Other Water* on 1 May. RC and Gallagher travel to England, where *Fires* and *The Stories of Raymond Carver* are published on 16 May. *Dostoevsky: A Screenplay*, co-authored by RC and Gallagher, is published in the fall by Capra Press. On 17 November, RC's review of two Hemingway biographies appears in the *New York Times Book Review*. That month, he also receives *Poetry* magazine's Levinson Prize.

1986   RC serves as guest editor of *The Best American Short Stories 1986*. Random House publishes his poetry collection *Ultramarine* on 7 November, the same day that RC and Gallagher are featured readers at the Modern Poetry Association's Poetry Day celebration in Chicago.

1987   On 3 April, Delacorte publishes *American Short Story Masterpieces*, edited by RC and Tom Jenks. In May, Raven Editions publishes *Those Days: Early Writings by Raymond Carver.* "Errand," RC's last published story, appears in *The New Yorker* on 1 June. From April to July, RC and Gallagher travel in Europe, visiting Paris, Wiesbaden, Zurich, Rome, and Milan. In London, Collins Harvill publishes *In a Marine Light*, a selection of Carver's recent poems, on 1 June. In September, RC experiences pulmonary hemorrhages, and on 1 October doctors in Syracuse remove two-thirds of his cancerous left lung. RC is inducted into the New York Public Library "Literary Lions" on 11 November. Guest editor Ann Beattie includes "Boxes" in *The Best American Short Stories 1987.*

1988   In January, RC buys a new house in Port Angeles. "Errand" is awarded first place in *Prize Stories 1988*, and guest editor Mark Helprin includes it in *The Best American Short Stories 1988.* RC serves as judge of *American Fiction 88.* In March, his cancer reappears, this time in the brain. During April and May, he undergoes a seven-week course of radiation treatments in Seattle. *Where I'm Calling From*, a major collection of his new and selected stories, is published in May by Atlantic Monthly Press. On 4 May, RC receives a Creative Arts Award Citation for Fiction from Brandeis University. On 15 May, he receives an honorary Doctor of Letters degree from the University of Hartford. On 18 May, he is inducted into the American Academy and Institute of Arts and Letters. In early June, cancer reappears in RC's lungs. He and Gallagher marry in Reno, Nevada, on 17 June. Working together, they assemble his last book of poetry, and in July they make a fishing trip to Alaska. After a brief stay in Virginia Mason Hospital in Seattle, RC dies at his new house in Port Angeles on 2 August at 6:20 a.m. He is buried in the Ocean View Cemetery in Port Angeles on 4 August, the same day that Collins Harvill publishes *Elephant and Other Stories* in London. RC's poem "Gravy" appears in *The New Yorker* on 29 August, and his essay "Friendship" is published in the autumn issue of *Granta.* A memorial service for him is held at Saint Peter's Church in New York City on 22 September.

1989   The Seattle Foundation awards its Maxine Cushing Gray Fellowship to Gallagher and, posthumously, to RC. Atlantic Monthly Press publishes RC's last book of poems, *A New Path to the Waterfall*, on 15 June. "Dreams Are What You Wake Up From," a BBC *Omnibus* documentary on RC's life and writing, is televised in England on 22 September. On 27 November, the English-Speaking Union confers its Ambassador Book Award on *Where I'm Calling From.*

Major Works by Raymond Carver and Tess Gallagher

Raymond Carver

Collected Stories. New York: Library of America, 2009.

Beginners: The Original Version of What We Talk About When We Talk About Love. London: Jonathan Cape, 2009; London: Vintage Books, 2010.

Call If You Need Me: The Uncollected Fiction and Prose. With a foreword by Tess Gallagher. London: Harvill Press, 2000; New York: Vintage Contemporaries, 2001.

All of Us: The Collected Poems. With an introduction by Tess Gallagher. London: Harvill Press, 1996; New York: Alfred A. Knopf, 1998; New York: Vintage Contemporaries, 2000.

Short Cuts: Selected Stories. With an introduction by Robert Altman. New York: Vintage Contemporaries, 1993.

No Heroics, Please: Uncollected Writings. With a foreword by Tess Gallagher. London: Harvill Press, 1991; New York: Vintage Contemporaries, 1992.

Carver Country: The World of Raymond Carver. With an introduction by Tess Gallagher and photographs by Bob Adelman. New York: Scribner's, 1990; New York: Arcade Publishing, 1994.

A New Path to the Waterfall. With an introduction by Tess Gallagher. New York: Atlantic Monthly Press, 1989.

Where I'm Calling From: New and Selected Stories. New York: Atlantic Monthly Press, 1988; New York: Vintage Contemporaries, 1989.

Ultramarine. New York: Random House, 1986; New York: Vintage Books, 1987.

Where Water Comes Together with Other Water. New York: Random House, 1985; New York: Vintage Books, 1986.

Cathedral. New York: Alfred A. Knopf, 1983; New York: Vintage Contemporaries, 1989.

Fires: Essays, Poems, Stories. Santa Barbara: Capra Press, 1983; expanded, New York: Vintage Contemporaries, 1989.

What We Talk About When We Talk About Love. New York: Alfred A. Knopf, 1981; New York: Vintage Contemporaries, 1989.

Furious Seasons and Other Stories. Santa Barbara: Capra Press, 1977. Out of print.

Will You Please Be Quiet, Please? New York: McGraw-Hill, 1976; New York: Vintage Contemporaries, 1992.

Tess Gallagher

Dear Ghosts. St. Paul: Graywolf Press, 2006.

Soul Barnacles: Ten More Years with Ray. Edited by Greg Simon. Ann Arbor: University of Michigan Press, 2000.

At the Owl Woman Saloon. New York: Scribner, 1997; Scribner Paperback, 1998.

My Black Horse: New and Selected Poems. Newcastle upon Tyne, England: Bloodaxe Books, 1995. Distributed in the U.S. by Dufour Editions.

Portable Kisses. Seattle: Sea Pen Press, 1978; Santa Barbara: Capra Press, 1992, expanded 1994; Newcastle upon Tyne, England: Bloodaxe Books, 1996. Distributed in the U.S. by Dufour Editions.

Moon Crossing Bridge. St Paul: Graywolf Press, 1992.

Amplitude: New and Selected Poems. St. Paul: Graywolf Press, 1987.

The Lover of Horses and Other Stories. New York: Harper & Row, 1986; Saint Paul: Graywolf Press, 1992.

A Concert of Tenses: Essays on Poetry. Ann Arbor: University of Michigan Press, 1986.

Willingly. Port Townsend, Wash.: Graywolf Press, 1984. Out of print.

Under Stars. Port Townsend, Wash.: Graywolf Press, 1978; St. Paul: Graywolf Press, 1988.

Instructions to the Double. Port Townsend, Wash.: Graywolf Press, 1976; Pittsburgh: Carnegie-Mellon University Press, 1997.

Raymond Carver and Tess Gallagher

Tell It All. Edited by William L. Stull and Maureen P. Carroll. Rome: Leconte, 2005.

Cattedrali / Cathedrals. Edited by Gianluca Bassi and Barbara Pezzopane. Rome: Leconte, 2002.

Dostoevsky: A Screenplay. Santa Barbara: Capra Press, 1985. Out of print.

This list of the major works by Raymond Carver and Tess Gallagher was compiled by William L. Stull and Maureen P. Carroll .